THE SEVEN
LAST WORDS
OF THE
CHURCH

THE SEVEN LAST WORDS OF THE CHURCH

Ralph W. Neighbour, Jr.

*Foreword by
Leighton Ford*

BROADMAN
Nashville, Tennessee

Acknowledgment is made to the following for use of copyrighted material:

OXFORD UNIVERSITY PRESS for quotations from *The New English Bible*. Copyright © 1961 by The Delegates of the Oxford University Press and The Syndics of the Cambridge University Press. All Scripture quotations are from *The New English Bible*.

GOOD NEWS PUBLISHERS, Westchester, Illinois 60153, for use of the tract, "Others May, You Cannot." Reprinted by permission.

Dewey Decimal Classification: 282.001
Subject heading: CHURCH RENEWAL
ISBN Number: 0-8054-5527-2
Library of Congress Catalog Card Number: 79–51937

Printed in the United States of America

This book is affectionately dedicated
to the people who have dared to call themselves
The People Who Care.

These are the words of the One who holds the seven stars in his right hand and walks among the seven lamps of gold: I know all your ways, your toil and your fortitude. . . . But I have this against you: you have lost your early love.

Revelation 2:1-4

Contents

Foreword

There is a kind of paradox about the way God works with men. His ways are *always old* and *always new*.

For example, in Isaiah 43:18 the Lord says, "Remember not the former things, nor consider the things of old. Behold, I am doing a new thing; now it springs forth, do you not perceive it?"(RSV). But then three chapters later He says, "Remember the former things of old; for I am God, and there is no other"!

I think the Lord is beginning to teach us in the church today that it's in the creative tension between the *always old* and the *always new* that He is working out His plans.

Ralph Neighbour is a man who understands this. And his book has helped me to feel this tension. As I read it, I felt all kinds of emotions. I wanted to laugh, cry, shout, argue, agree, debate, shout "Hallelujah," and run away.

Those who read this book may not agree with everything that's said. But I think all of us ought to murmur a deep "Thank God" for pioneers like Ralph Neighbour who are able to live on the cutting edge of the ways of God.

Some people are saying the way to church renewal today is simply to develop "new wineskins." If I understand what Ralph Neighbour is saying, it's that first we have to start with "the new wine"—the Gospel of the death and resurrect.on of our Lord Jesus Christ and the new birth He brings—and the real ferment of this profound change of conversion then must be expressed in "the new wineskins."

One thing I'd especially like to note. Those who

9

have been led to experiment with new ways often write with a kind of disdain for the "old fogies" who lag so far behind them. I don't catch this note of superiority or condescension in this book. Ralph Neighbour has a profound gratitude for the great things which God has done in the past and continues to do through traditional forms in the church. He sees their value but he also sees that we have to have those persons who are willing to pay the price of moving ahead in the new things, to make some mistakes, to admit them, and, as God's "point men" to find some new paths which the Holy Spirit is blazing for us.

LEIGHTON FORD

Charlotte, N.C.

Introduction

Words are such fickle things! They wax and wane with the mobility of High Fashion, moving in and out of style as rapidly as the width of men's neckties. Moreover, like women's skirt lengths, they often reflect the spirit of their time. In the fashion language of religion, the "in words" now include: *renewal, authentic, valid, relevant,* and *truly redemptive.*

Those words reveal a desperate desire by many Christians to rediscover a fresh, vigorous life of faith that does not have to be "faked" before a skeptical, humanistic society. They are words which admit the church is in trouble, that it includes insincerity, powerlessness, and ineffectiveness.

We are told the church needs "renewal"!

Earlier generations who struggled with these same problems spoke of the need for "revival." Some of those generations, unlike ours, *actually did experience* the fresh breath of God within their midst, making their witness of a transforming Christ "authentic, valid, relevant, and truly redemptive."

Somehow, the old shopworn word "revival" is not sophisticated enough for today's erudite generation. To many nonevangelicals, it does not permit enough width within the theological spectrum. Those who speak of revival are often considered the radical fringe, who still believe in such "archaic concepts" as an authoritative Scripture, a Christ literally born of a virgin, etc. A new word is needed for the Modern, one which will permit a range of theology which soars from Robinson to Bultmann.

"Renewal" is the word!

The church needs *renewal,* not *revival.* It is hiding

behind brick walls and stained glass windows! It needs to return its ministry to the laity! It needs a renewed theology! The answer lies in a new program twist, in a new structure for the church! So we are told.

Because fashionable words sell books, suggestions about renewal from armchair generals who have never fought a battle have been flying about for some time. Exotic ideas concerning restructuring everything or even abandoning the old institutional church are in print. Some suggest that the key to renewal is simply to toughen membership requirements or to expand the level of the layman's theological awareness of *ecclesia*. Some clairvoyants have dreamed up the church of A.D. 1999 and have written startling portrayals of what it is going to be like:

This volume is written by a minister who has attempted to live with other believers in one expression of the renewed life of the church. He shares in the experimental life of the West Memorial Baptist Church of Houston, a theologically conservative, radically "renewed" congregation. It will be described in the pages to follow. The important lessons which are now being discovered by "The People Who Care" who live in Houston is the stuff of these pages.

The supreme lesson we have learned is this: *Renewal cannot begin through any of the above methods.* It must originate through a body of believers who understand that they exist in an age in which the Holy Spirit has, to a large extent, withdrawn His presence. They must be aware that our Lord Jesus Christ is standing in the shadows beside this ridiculous world scene, patiently waiting for His Little Children to put away their silly, religious toys and programs and discover that He has come to control their mundane, pressured existences. *Renewal, after all, is revival!* It is a deeply personal thing and involves much more pain and far more commitment than most renewalists seem willing to endure.

THE SEVEN LAST WORDS OF THE CHURCH

PART ONE

THE PEOPLE WHO CARE

1

The Seven Last Words of the Church

Turtles are displayed in symbol and in fact on the hillsides and house sides of Okinawa. Rooted in the ancient centuries when the island was a part of China, the turtle has symbolized both fertility (shaped like a womb) and long life (they seem to live forever!). Lovely modern golf courses include as "obstacles" turtle-shaped stone tombs, and virtually every home displays a taxidermied specimen in the main room.

Upon a sunny morning, I spied an aged man snoozing on a wooden stool at the side of Naha's busiest thoroughfare. On the street beside him were the primitive tools he used to put new heels on old shoes. His pitiful "store" could be carried away under his arm at the end of the day. His business was poor; consequently, he had drawn up one leg under his chair and was soundly snoring. Beside him, swimming in an old and rusted coffee can, was a small turtle. It might have been a sign of fertility and longevity to the Oriental, but what impressed this Yankee at the moment was its ceaseless activity. You see, that coffee can of water gave no opportunity for the turtle to quit swimming! There was no resting place in it—no stone or shallow section where the turtle could snooze beside his master. While the old man slept, his "lucky piece" struggled to keep from drowning.

I photographed the scene because I saw humor in the situation. Lately, however, my slide has become a symbol to me of a terrifying, nightmarish situation faced by the church. The old, snoring man symbolizes quite well the attitude of much of the church in today's world. We have the barest possible collection of Spirit-given tools available to aid us in our task of "re-soul-ing" the unbeliever who comes to us, and in our day we are asleep to a passing population which desperately needs our help. At our feet, fighting to keep from drowning in the waters of change, is a fertile and aging culture of a world which is doubling its population in just a handful of years. How humorous we in the church must look to the strolling tourist who glances at us! We are old, we are asleep, we are not even sure of our "place" in the markets of this earth. We are not anxious to observe the opportunities to repair the needs of people who pass us by. We tend to feel subconsciously that our struggling American culture is for us a turtle of good luck; after all, have we not stamped on our coins "In God We Trust"? Good old America is godly, even if it is swimming frantically in the waters of change. We need not be disturbed. The gates of hell cannot prevail against us. Why all the fuss about our need to change? Everything will turn out all right. Everybody knows from the last chapter in the Book that God is going to win. As long as the bills are paid and members don't fuss, we in the church need not be too disturbed by the alarmists who keep shouting for us to change or die.

And so, we have coined our *Seven Last Words:* "We never tried it that way before!" We say them when someone suggests the Gospel does not require sanctuaries. We repeat them when we are told Sunday school may one day be replaced by Bible studies which meet in kitchens, that committed Christians might more effectively witness on Sunday evenings by decentralizing their worship services into cells across the community. We spit these words out with venom when new forms of church music appear or when our youth suggest to us that building gymnatoriums is much more sensible than building auditoriums.

Satan has always been a genius at discovering the weakest points in God's children and seeking to destroy them by an attack where the least resistance will be encountered. In individual believers, he may attack through the thin walls surrounding lust, jealousy, greed, or hatred. In the contemporary church, he has found the easiest entrée through our fear of losing more and more ground in our shifting society. Those scared souls who cling to their security rather than dare to follow the Spirit keep crying out, "Danger! *We never tried it that way before!*" They seem to react in a fleshly fear to God's demand to forsake all and follow Him. Good old Abraham might have been right to leave lands and friends to follow God to a city whose builder and maker He was, but he had only *barbarians* with whom to contend. We must protect our church properties and budgets, our hierarchical structures and boards, our publication agencies and near-pagan colleges. He had nothing but bare land to leave behind him, with a few goats grazing on it—it's not the same today. We must strive to protect our investments. Beware of the Spirit! His call to rapid change and ministry to *outsiders* must surely interfere with our five-year development programs, our salary structures, our seminary curriculums, and retirement benefits. Let some fool idiot move into experimental structures; the wise man relies on the old and tested ways.

Yesterday I spoke three times at an evangelism conference sponsored by about a hundred churches. (I am always fascinated by the courage of lay men

17

and women to expose their brains and bodies to no less than nine sermons in a period of twelve hours during one of these marathons of exhortation!) One of the preliminary preachers had heard me speak before and was aware of my feelings regarding the urgent need for the church to get on with change. Less than ten minutes of his message had been delivered when I began to feel furtive eyes glancing my way to observe my reaction to his message. The dear brother was tearing down in advance every point he expected me to present in the main address. He was red-facedly insisting that the "church" was many things to many people, *including a building and a program!* His vituperation reminded me for a moment of some of the phlegmatic diatribes delivered by St. Jerome against a friend or two he devastatingly dissected during a decade of heated, hating debate. At that precise moment, I quit listening to his words and began to hear objectively the emotions he was erupting.

This dear pastor was running scared! He was totally threatened by the suggestion of the new, the changed. His emotion was not that of hatred, but of terror. He was not speaking "in the Spirit," but "in the flesh." I reached out in love to him from the audience, for he was a symbol of all those who are asleep while the turtle frantically swims. To be aroused from sound slumber by the explosion of a backfiring truck or a loud crescendo is upsetting! The entire psyche is disturbed. The reactions include fear, irritation, anger, frustration, defensiveness, or aggressiveness. I determined to react to this seeming public attack in the only Christian way available. When the message was completed and we had been dismissed, I spoke with great love to him, thanking him for a message that he obviously had labored over for many hours. Together, we walked to the cafeteria for lunch, and I asked him about his family and his church. At that lunch table we shared intimately our dreams and our problems, and left friends indeed. He did not need to be debated. He needed to be *loved;* our Lord has taught us that love alone can cast out fear.

The following chapters are presented with the strong conviction that the afraidlike quality of today's churchmen facing change will be conquered by Christ's love alone. Christ reassuringly says to us, "Do not be afraid. Lo, I am with you. The valley of change may seem dark, but My rod and staff will comfort you. Listen only in the darkness for the sounds of the Shepherd's tapping-out-the-way staff. You are living in a place where the grass is brown and withered. I wish to lead you into the green pastures of My perfect will. Fear not! My love will guide the way. True, you have never tried this way before, but *I* know where we are going. Walk by faith, not sight. Remember, the seven *first* words of the church are *'I can do all things through Christ!'* "

> *This* is not the future's first verse!
> Always it keeps coming—at supersonic speeds.
> Suddenly in the desert stands
> John the Baptist.
> "Repent!" he shouts,
> "The future—*God's* future—is at hand!"
> It will not wait
> And so Jesus comes.
> Are we ready?
> Do we welcome Him?
> Do we love Him?
> Do we serve Him?
> Do we see Him for who He is?
> Or do we go on, hating the Romans,
> Talking about the price of eggs?
> Still the future speeds;
> Tomorrow starts today.
> People move.
> Cities grow.
> Times change.
> In the name of God, we must do better than before!
> The future will not wait!
>
> —Author unknown

2

The Beginning of a Dream

Among the greatest disappointments Ruth and I have faced was our physician's conclusion that her health would make it impossible for us to be appointed as missionaries. Our world tumbled in around us!

Throughout seminary we had lived, breathed, and toiled for the day when we could sail away for a lifetime of overseas service. My chosen field for postgraduate studies had been missions; my thesis topic, "The People Movement Method of Missions."

We had not even considered the *possibility* that our lives might be lived out within the United States! Now we found ourselves "locked in"—in spite of the fact that since our early teens we both had felt God's call to "the mission field."

For a month after the doctor talked to us, we just couldn't bring ourselves to discuss future plans. One day, while we were on our knees together, God finally seemed to answer our "Why?" by saying, "My children, two thousand miles of salt water won't make a missionary! You must begin to understand that *every person who belongs to Me is commissioned to be a minister,* and every unreached life on the face of this globe constitutes a mission field!"

We then volunteered our lives for service through the work of the Home Mission Board. Through a dizzying series of events, we soon found ourselves in the heart of Pennsylvania as "home missionaries."

Five years later we had helped to start new churches in Pennsylvania, New Jersey, New York, and Connecticut, and had moved three times. More important, we began to realize that *one of the greatest untapped mission fields in the world remained in the United States!*

I am referring to the "mission field" of unchurched, pagan, couldn't-care-less Americans who gave up religion a generation or more ago. They are to be found from the Atlantic to the Pacific and represent an ever-growing percentage of the American population. They literally live in the shadow of church buildings; yet churches are not even able to *communicate* successfully with them!

Our mission field was to become the nonchurch-oriented Americans we began to call "the outsiders." What a serendipity it was to find them in our own homeland! We had as difficult a time trying to relate to the "natives" of our mission field as we might have had with the Bantus of Africa. Our outsiders spoke a different language, for one thing. (Ruth and I had both been raised in deeply devout Christian homes.) For another thing, there was the problem of their acceptance of us. We clearly did not "belong" to their society. Their customs, traditions, thought patterns, and social customs were radically new to us and required a great deal of adjustment on our part.

When I excitedly began to share the news of our mission field with my pastor friends, I discovered that few of them (in those years) even recognized the existence of outsiders! For example, I well recall visiting with a pastor in a West Florida town. I asked him what his church did to reach the unchurched who would never choose to visit his worship services. He replied, "Why, I hardly have time to visit the

21

people who visit us on Sunday morning. Honestly, I am too busy trying to reach those who *do* worship with us to worry about those who don't come around."

But then, the early sixties were those days of rapidly growing congregations, of "successes" in church expansion. These accomplishments blinded many pastors to what was happening even then under our noses: people in America were quietly relegating the church to a secondary position in their lives. Those who did so by "skipping" services because "company from out-of-town came in for the weekend" gave a clue to what was happening, but for the most part these "dropouts" were considered by churchmen to be something like irritating mosquitoes.

The problem of outsiders was ignored. Church leaders should have recognized that the "out-of-towners" who kept church members at home were waving the future at them. Instead, clergymen thought, *Who are these horrible pagans from some far-distant town who disrupted our sedate religious environment in our godly community with their disturbing presence?*

They were the outsiders. That they were outside the church was simply an irritation in the early sixties; no effort was made to reach them.

Suddenly, the outsiders exploded into a dominant group within our culture. The camping grounds of America were suddenly filled with millions of people who began to live in tents and trailers for the weekend. Without thought of church, the American public in ever-increasing numbers had "turned to its own way," and the mission field we recognized thirteen years ago began to grow faster than anything the church had had to cope with in nineteen centuries.

In the middle 1960's our family moved to the Southwest, where I had been invited to serve in the Evangelism Division of the Baptist General Convention of Texas. We found the outsiders in Texas, too! When we arrived, we found an alive church, teeming with choirs and activities, doing a splendid job of reaching the insiders, but still barely recognizing even the existence of the outsiders.

For several years a gnawing pain in my heart kept increasing in intensity. From the vantage point of serving within a denominational position, I saw that our leadership was so pressured to meet deadlines that deep thought and creativity was nearly impossible. It was also obvious that pastors were running at such a dizzy pace that they did not see the outsiders, let alone have time to pray about God's strategy for ministering to them.

The nights became increasingly sleepless as God kept saying to me, "Ralph, why don't you recognize that *I have called you to be a missionary?* The field is all around you! You must find my ways for reaching outsiders. You must find the new life I have for God's family, which will be able to help them reach these unreached ones. You *must accept* the mandate I have for your life and move into the realm of the experimental way with me. *I want you to be a pioneer missionary to the outsiders.*"

It took six years of struggle for me to answer that call! During that period, I wrote to a friend at the Home Mission Board,

> It is impossible to conceive of a major industry, such as General Electric or Westinghouse, operating without a Research and Development staff. This, however, is precisely what our churches are doing at the present time. A great deal is being done to refine the old methods, but not one official group within the denomination has had the courage to say, "Let's experiment with new forms of the church. From such research, perhaps exciting new patterns will be discovered which may far outstrip the old ones in reaching Outsiders for conversion, growth, and involvement in God's work."

By 1968, I began to feel that the only way such research and development could ever be attempted would be on the local church level. Current denominational structures were fairly well projected through the end of the 1970's, and they continued to move in a synthesis of old patterns. Someone had to be willing to lead out, to pay the price of really innovative research and experiment, or we would still be floundering in the 1980's with rural concepts of the church—concepts that might well bankrupt us by 1985! There seemed to be limited courage among denominational agencies to project a frankly experimental church which would be a guinea pig for research. Nevertheless, within every single agency there were important, creative men who encouraged me by sharing suggestions for the development of an experimental group. They admitted the need and welcomed the attempt.

Gradually our dream took shape on paper. I began to write about a totally committed group, ready to dare to *be* totally committed, anxious to seek the power of the Holy Spirit which might lead to a "great awakening," ready to serve Jesus Christ completely, to lead separated lives, to experiment, to have the "courage to fail."

Little did I know, then, *how much courage* failure would require and in how personal a way I would discover that for myself!

The initial proposals I wrote down suggested that the experimental group include these details if at all possible:

1. The minister would have to be promoted from being a "star quarterback" on the playing field to being Trueblood's "player-coach."[1] He should be more interested in seeing the laymen grow and become equipped for ministry than in attracting people to Christ by his own personal dynamic.

2. *Evangelism* would have to be the life-force of the group—but *not* evangelism in the sense of meetings where a preacher preached and an audience lis-

---

[1] See Elton Trueblood's *The Incendiary Fellowship* (New York: Harper and Row, 1967).

tened. It must be evangelism in the way Daniel T. Niles defined it: "One hungry beggar telling another hungry beggar where to find bread."

3. The target area must be outsiders—the totally unchurched, the hardest group in our society to reach. This would mean abandoning, to a large extent, the investment of time spent in visiting active church members who would move into the community. Available hours would be invested in relating to outsiders.

4. Even though presently used methods might work perfectly, this new congregation would not use them to any great extent. Their frank task should be to find new ways to reach outsiders. The congregation should rejoice in what might work for other churches, but remain in a position where it could constantly test *new concepts*. This would be our "gift of love" to sister churches: to try and fail and try and succeed, so that fellow soldiers might learn new ways from our experiment.

5. Deacons would be structured around the shepherding of the flock. They would have no tasks at all except those acts of loving, caring, counseling, and guiding the members in spiritual matters.

6. Deacons would serve as leaders for *retreats,* which would be envisioned as an opportunity for church members to really get to know each other— and to get down to brass tacks with the heavenly Father about becoming involved in their ministries.

7. The *Church* would be the "called-out ones"— the "family of God"—and the word would not be used to describe a building.

8. The group should learn to function without buildings. They would be aware that in the full stewardship of Christ, all they possess actually belongs to Jesus Christ. Further, all homes would be much closer to the scene of ministering to outsiders than a traditional church building. Members would utilize their homes to the fullest extent for Christ.

9. In order to reach out, the group would commit

itself to the primary proclamation of Christ as Lord, rather than to an organization, a denomination, or a limited theology. Having reached outsiders for the Master, they would then seek to bring these new believers into the ministry of the group, with all that this involved.

10. The congregation would basically be a "disciple factory"—reaching, equipping, sending—so that new believers might quickly become a part of the ministry. Further, the children of members would be involved in ministries at the earliest possible age.

Could such a group exist within a setting of traditional churches? Could adults, raised in another form of church life, make the overwhelming transition required to live in this new structure? I asked myself these questions over and over again for two years.

Another question developed: Could my own theology, conservative without apology, apply to a radically changing form of the church? There were those who suggested that my old theology would not fit into the new wineskin. I disagreed. My theology would remain conservative, unchanged. (Little did I know that, to some, church structure *was* theology; I was hardly prepared for the later accusations that I was a "liberal." I was to become the first premillennial "liberal" in history!)

Ruth and I began to struggle with the final plans for beginning such a work. A dear and trusted friend at our Home Mission Board felt some recognition could be given to the experiment by his department, thus giving it official sanction. Several men at the Sunday School Board expressed an interest in the project and volunteered unofficial assistance in terms of becoming a "brain trust." Many other colleagues did not understand my concerns or were threatened by it all, and they openly attacked the concept of an experimental church as being "too radical."

We began to pray about the people who might

enter into such a life with us. Could any existing group see the challenge?

A telephone call came from a friend, indicating that a new congregation in a large city would like me to come and talk with them about pastoring there. My visit to the group included an explanation of what I felt called to do. A cloud of shock settled upon them, and long before our Sunday fellowship was over, I realized just *how* threatening my concepts had been to these "typical" Christian laymen.

As a result, I had just about decided the only way to get the experiment off the ground would be to meet long-term outsiders, reach them for Christ, and use them to begin the work. I had given up on the possibility of finding Christians raised in traditional structures who would be able to live with the strain of the new life.

Perhaps, I thought, the Lord will require me for the first time in my life to "leave the ministry" temporarily in order that I might reach a core of outsiders. Perhaps a position as a counselor in a large university would be the answer . . . perhaps there I could find some twenty-year-old "pagans" and introduce them to Christ. It might take six to ten years to develop a nucleus in this way, but it would be a start!

3

The Beginning of 'The People Who Care'

The endless months of thinking, planning, and writing finally culminated in the revealing of God's pattern for the experimental church. Like many other acts of God, the details were so simple when they happened that we almost couldn't believe it!

In January of 1969, an invitation came for me to preach to a small fellowship of Christians in Houston. They had been meeting in a rented school building for a few weeks, and as yet they had no sense of direction for their future. Located in the affluent West Memorial section of the city, the group felt a church needed to be established there, even though no encouragement had been provided by local officials of the denomination. Further, they had been very loosely "sponsored" by another church which made it clear that the new congregation could expect neither financial help nor members from the mother congregation.

My visit with the group excited me. These were deeply committed Christians who had a true pioneering spirit. Could they share my vision, or would they run away, as had the former church group? Our conversations together that Sunday led me to feel that this band of believers came closer to being ready for an experimental structure than any other group I had met in years. I boarded my plane that night with a silent prayer that God might show me—and them—His will, if indeed we were to serve Him together.

Everything seemed right. The group had not yet shaped its goals. The members were creative. There were no "strangleholds" on them by a parent body. The community in which they were located was destined to be a sea of apartment houses, truly the outsider's "world of tomorrow." They *could* be God's plan for the new "Research and Development Center." If so, the Lord would have to open the door for us to talk again. I left all the details with Him.

I returned to Houston in April, 1969, to conduct a city-wide Personal Evangelism Institute. Almost immediately a representative from the fellowship approached me about becoming pastor of the group. My full confession of intent regarding church structure had not scared them away—but I still had doubts about how well they understood the experimental life I had in mind.

With their encouragement, I prepared a fifty-nine page manuscript which thoroughly detailed *The Dream*. Copies of it were duplicated for their pulpit committee for study prior to a scheduled conference to discuss the details. Excerpts from it said,

All I write has been written from the conviction that the "Church" was meant by Jesus Christ to be a redemptive fellowship, rather than a religious equivalent of secular promotion.

It is important to remember while reading the proposals set forth that this entire paper is intended to be a "guidebook" rather than a "rulebook." It is hoped that the thoughts within might be used to discover a more biblical and contemporary concept of the Church. However, the final structure of the local church should be the joint work of a creative body of Christians who intend to give their lives to make it work. The basic *substance* of the Church outlined might possibly be activized in significantly changed form from the *procedure* suggested! If basic agreement on the *substance* is present, the *procedure* may be subjected to the most serious scrutiny and changed from that suggested in this paper. However, there must be a starting point for discussion. This paper is written to provide that starting point.

How does one reduce a dream to a printed text? A totally committed group, ready to dare to *be* totally committed, anxious to seek the power of the Holy Spirit which might lead to a Great Awakening, ready to completely serve Jesus Christ, and to lead separated lives, are at the heart of this experiment. Does your group have the courage to be a part of it?

Dwight L. Moody overheard the conversation of two Christian women one day. One said to the other, "The world has yet to see what God can do with a man fully dedicated to Him." On his knees, Dwight L. Moody said, "I will be that man." He put one hand on America, the other on England, and pushed both of those nations beneath the shadow of the Cross. His name will be forever revered.

The time has come when we must realize that our Lord is saying, "The world has yet to see what I can do with a church fully committed to Me." Have we the courage to dare to be that church?

Once the laity realizes that there is no other force in the Church that can work at the grass roots for constructive change, once they realize it is within their power to demonstrate what honest Christians *can* do for God in today's world, once they prove that they *can* be spiritually matured and effectively "go and disciple others," other restless churches will, to varying degrees, follow this example. Once these things occur, the tide of irrelevance may turn, and⸠a God-breathed movement may develop.

We have passed through a period in the life of the Church in which the vital expression of the Gospel has declined to a hollow shell of what our grandparents knew. It is time to teach, to preach, to reach once more a world that ignores Christ's claims because of the form of the Church. It is time that Jesus Christ be mocked (by the world) for the right reasons.

This is an age of unbelievable change. Everything is in the process of change. Society as well as technology has been thrown into transition. In spite of this, the Church continues to propagate itself, using a system and a program which has remained virtually unchanged in its basic conceptions for seventy-five years.

There is much less risk in changing the pattern of the

Church than in *not* changing. To the thoughtful Christian, it is not sufficient that the present structure works or that it is a comfortable compromise. The real question is whether it is the best we can devise to reach today's world with the unsearchable message of Jesus Christ.

The local church today may be at a dead end not because it is totally irrelevant, but because it still assumes that the few "bright spots" may somehow compensate for the structural weakness of the whole. For the few "bright spots" on the horizon—churches in plush suburbs which are still growing—there are hundreds of others who are steadily declining.

A contemporary society competes brutally with the program of the Church. The public school is no longer a place where reading, writing, and arithmetic are being taught. Its competitive force is felt by virtually all congregations. Color television has forever removed the gimmick of "entertainment" as a useful tool of church evangelism.

Yet, we continue to build ranch-style church buildings on three or more acres of land, in spite of the fact that land now costs $80,000 per acre in the "right" location in an urban area. We need the buildings to house programs that are constantly losing impact.

All these factors call the Church of Tomorrow to enclose these principles in its structure:

1. Its requirements for membership must be biblical, not "practical." It must be an act of integrity to belong to the church.

2. It should begin with a "Thus-saith-the-Lord" theology. A church cannot continually worry about doctrine and also concentrate on the task of evangelizing a lost world. Its theology should focus upon changing men, not the structures of society.

3. Its "Standard of Success" should be: (a) Are we bringing the unbeliever to a personal commitment to Jesus Christ? (b) Are we developing that believer to a place where he is *totally consumed* with Christ's indwelling presence? (c) Are we involving our members in effective "pre-evangelism" contacts with the community's unbelievers? Are we reaching out, or are we a "country club"?

4. Its property should be functional, utilitarian, *and disposable!*

5. Its budget and program should focus upon ministering to unbelievers. Perhaps 80% of its activity and 50% of its budget would be devoted to this purpose.

6. It should be willing to scrutinize itself ruthlessly to

31

discover nonproductive functions, and perform radical surgery on its appendaged programs.

7. It must come to some carefully discussed conclusions about its standards for personal living in a secular world. Let the church study biblical principles, and be guided by them—regardless of who condones or criticizes. Let it discover the full meaning of "sanctification" —a people "set apart"—and usable by the Holy Spirit.

8. Let it believe in prayer, practice prayer, learn to pray, teach to pray. The contemporary church has made a hollow mockery of prayer. Let it begin where the 120 began—"tarrying for power." Tomorrow's Church must, MUST, *MUST* be born and borne of the Spirit, in the manner of the Church during the Great Awakening. Today's Church strives to do the work of God without His presence! Before it becomes consumed in *doing,* let it learn to blaze with *Being.* From the outset, it must view "worship" as a direct encounter *with* God, not a discussion *about* Him. Until this "lost chord" is recaptured, the sounds of the church will be tinkling brass, sounding cymbals.

The major purpose for keeping the church unstructured at the start is so that the *true* leadership of the Spirit can first be discovered. *Then* let the people follow His leadership in the activity of the church.

Delay is due to our unwillingness, not to God's reluctance. He *wants* to fill His Church! Most Christians I talk to about this, however, do not even understand what I mean. Something not known previously is hard to experience.

Twelve hours of dialogue followed their reading of this paper, with the pulpit committee deeply impressed by the possibilities. We agreed together, however, that only the first twenty pages of the document should be shared with the entire group, thus allowing more freedom for them to participate in the development of the actual structure we would use.

To emphasize my firm commitment to the experimental structure, I refused to allow them to discuss any financial arrangements regarding salary, indicating that my *sole interest* was their willingness to relate to our new way of life. As a result, our family was willing to come to Houston prepared to take part-time employment if necessary. (The little congregation was

32

more than generous to us, however, in the matter of salary, and we were able to serve them on a full-time basis from the beginning.)

In June of 1969, we met with the entire congregation of thirty-five or forty, and a few days later we formally committed ourselves to each other.

At this time, the Department of Metropolitan Missions of our Home Mission Board recognized us officially, providing limited endorsement for our activity. In addition, the Baptist Sunday School Board encouraged the congregation to permit me to spend my first month as their pastor in Nashville, Tennessee, and promised guided study to better equip me for our pilgrimage. With the Home Mission Board providing the expenses for this sabbatical, the offer was accepted.

My month in Nashville still remains in my memory as the most fruitful and productive investment of time I have ever known! Dr. W. O. Thomasson spent many hours, often stretching beyond midnight, challenging my thoughts about our structure. Assigned readings in Toynbee and many other authors, both published and unpublished, alerted me to the problems connected with radical change. During one period of six days and nights I remained in my hotel room—writing, thinking, praying, and occasionally sleeping.

When I finally caught my plane for Houston, a sixty-one-page document was in my briefcase, detailing a proposed life structure for our group. It would be studied for the next sixteen weeks and changed over and over as the entire membership grappled with the details of our new life.

Of primary importance in the document was the recommendation that we minister to outsiders in the name of "The People Who Care," laying little stress upon the words "Baptist" or "Church." It was felt that these two words would unnecessarily alienate unbelievers who had missed meeting Christ through prejudice against the structured church. We would eliminate nearly all "come structures" in favor of a "go structure."

"TOUCH" was to be the ministry of outreach, the "go structure" of The People Who Care. The word stands for "Transforming Others Under Christ's Hand." Even as other churches organized "come structures" by using names like "Training Union" or "Woman's Missionary Union," we would organize our outreach to outsiders under the name of "TOUCH" ministries.

Perhaps the analogy is ridiculous, but I felt a great deal like Abraham must have felt at the time he left Ur of the Chaldees to find "a city whose builder and maker was God." The dream of a church which would be built and made by the Holy Spirit was about to become reality! But I wonder if Abraham felt as lonely as I did as I flew over Tennessee. I had just "cut the strings" with the comfortable security of the structured church and even with my new-found friends in Nashville who bade me Godspeed.

I pushed the loneliness away by beginning to memorize the names and addresses of my little flock in Houston.

4

Excerpts From 'The Red Book'

This chapter presents the highlights of the suggested "go structures" contained in the sixty-one-page document written in Nashville.

I. *The Changing Contemporary Church*

Victor Hugo said, "No army can withstand the strength of an idea whose time has come." The idea that present organizations are no longer "sacred" has come to Southern Baptists. Structures are in transition from the top to bottom of Convention existence. For the first time, separate agencies are undergoing self-imposed discipline to correct the proliferation of programs that literally swamp the local church.

> It is not unusual to find that major changes in life ... break the patterns of our lives and reveal to us quite suddenly how much we had been imprisoned by the comfortable web we had woven around ourselves. Unlike the jailbird, we don't know that we've been imprisoned until after we've broken out.[1]

A. *The Purpose for Change*

A church should not change just to be different. It

---

[1] John W. Gardner, *Self-Renewal* (New York: Harper & Row, 1964) p. 9.

should change because the context of culture about it requires its organizations to restructure themselves so church tasks can be effectively fulfilled. It is important to recognize that "change generally alters the less important, the form and circumstances, the setting and surroundings, and the instrument and conditions of life. Seldom does change alter the essence of life. . . ."[2]

Change, then, is seen to be *a means to making the old truths more influential in a new environment*. This, and this alone, should be the underlying philosophy in recommending changes in church life.

B. *Reasons for Change at West Memoral Baptist Church*

The following reasons undergird the "model for change" set forth in this paper:

1. Our group is capable of change where other groups are not. We have no structures, no programs, no financial obligations for buildings created to house existing organizations.

2. Our community will require radically different outreach approaches in witness and ministry. We are set in an area destined to be a sea of apartment houses and better-than-average-priced homes. Traditional forms of visitation and revivals will not effectively reach the unchurched, although they would probably attract the Baptists in the area. If we intend to proclaim the truth of Christ's redemption realistically, we must have a significantly different form of outreach.

3. A significantly different form of outreach will require a significantly different form of training and study. Curriculum materials which do not lend themselves to our objectives in outreach would be a millstone about our necks. Organizational structures which

---

2 W. L. Howse and W. O. Thomasson, *A Dynamic Church* (Nashville: Convention Press, 1969), pp. 11, 12.

are not deliberately geared to prepare us and to carry out our tasks effectively would also be stumbling blocks.

4. A changing world requires different tools to accomplish old objectives. A perfect example of this is the Woman's Missionary Union. It began to teach missions, to study about missions, to create a burden for the evangelization of the lost in heathen lands, to secure funds for missions, and to challenge young people to follow God's call to the mission field. It was developed as an organization in an age when it was financially and transportationally impossible for the average church member to visit a mission field. Slides and mission study books replaced such trips. Today, however, it is a relatively inexpensive matter to go by jet to a foreign field or by auto to a home mission field. By placing ourselves on a triennial basis *on* a mission field and by spending a year in preparation for the experience, the need of missions will come alive in a fashion that the traditional approach cannot equal!

5. God has given us an opportunity—and responsibility—to be the instigator of a subculture of change. The greatest gift, and the most loyal act we can perform for the church at this point in history, is to create a divergent pattern of organization which is so logical that, once we have proved its feasibility, others will choose to adopt it.

Underlying our desire to be a subculture is, of course, a major objective of our church life: to win all men everywhere to faith in Jesus Christ. The more we can do to stem the tide of witnessless irrelevance in our denomination and the more we can influence other churches to "get where the action is," the more redemptive the church will become!

II. *Underlying Principles of the Proposed Model*

A. *Is Intended as a Guide*. The model presented in this paper is to be used only as a guide. As with our church objectives, the membership itself must be responsible for seeking the direction of the Holy Spirit in creating the actual model we shall adopt.

B. *Assumes Total Involvement.* This proposed structure is predicated on the conviction that each member desires to proclaim the Good News, using the unique gifts provided by God. It is designated to provide a context in which genuine proclamation is not only possible, but is the razor edge of the life of the Church. Indeed, all that takes place in this model focuses upon inspiring, maturing, training, and educating the member for his task of proclamation. *It has deliberately rejected all use of program, curriculum, organization, meetings, committees, or expenditures which do not specifically focus upon preparation for outreach, or outreach itself.*

C. *Emphasizes Koinonia.* Purely "social" activity has been replaced with *koinonia.* It provides opportunities for Christians to minister in love to the needs of each other. It provides opportunities for worship to be dynamic, not just a denominational ritual which varies only in sermon content.

D. *Is to Place the Church in the World.* Above all, this model is developed with the conviction that the church needs to be squarely in the world of human need, committed to the teaching of the Scriptures, and deeply involved in sharing a Gospel that transcends all of culture and is Good News to all men.

E. *Shrinks From Buildings.* Finally, it is developed on the principle that buildings are a necessary evil to the life of the church. Building costs and land values have been kept in mind, as well as the strong likelihood that churches will be taxed within fifteen years. The lifeblood of the Church is seen as flowing through *people,* not the arteries of educational building halls.

III. *Proposed Model and Traditional Organizations*

The illustrated model continues all present emphasis of a typical church, but with a new structure. *The structure is required by the objective to reach outsiders*

38

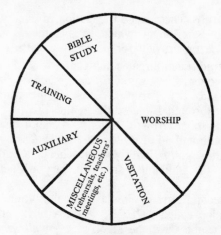

PRESENT INVESTMENT OF WEEKLY TIME
TYPICAL CHURCH

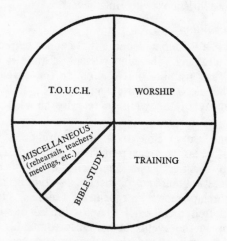

PROPOSED INVESTMENT OF WEEKLY TIME
MODEL CHURCH

39

redemptively. There is no dissipation of energy, study, or time in doing things which do not prepare members for service or provide for personal growth.

The traditional organizations are to be found in the new ones. For example, *Sunday school* has been divided into two parts: the first is the training of believers through Bible study in the *Training Center* and at *Personal Growth Retreats.* A major change reduces youth and adult Bible study in the *Training Center* to *four* groups, with *four* teachers. "Grading" is done by the individual and will vary with spiritual growth.

The second part of Sunday school is found in the organization called *TOUCH,* where a high percentage of the members will be involved in *small group discussions of Bible passages with unbelievers in homes.* Thus, Bible study becomes study *for* Christians and study *by* Christians with unbelievers.

IV. *Scheduling*

Time is a valuable resource that cannot be reclaimed if used unwisely. The management of time is an important responsibility of a church. In the development of a schedule, the requirements of each activity and the integrity of the whole enterprise should be considered.

Present use of time by many churches is one of the most pressing areas requiring renovation! A vexing factor for members and church staff members alike is the incessant demand for meetings—committee meetings, worship services, rehearsals, socials, etc. The active church member is literally forced out of participation in the events of his culture and his society so that he can attend the services and activities of his church! If the church is to be "in the world," then the church must stop meeting four nights out of seven. Family, community, and occupational contexts provide opportunities for witness and ministry. Members cannot make an impact on their society if

40

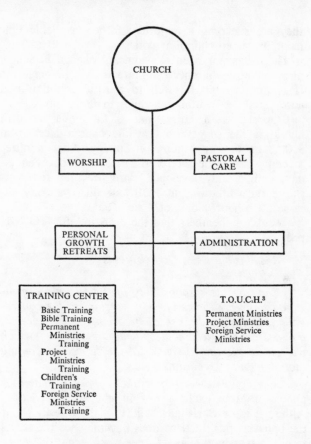

CHURCH

WORSHIP

PASTORAL CARE

PERSONAL GROWTH RETREATS

ADMINISTRATION

TRAINING CENTER
Basic Training
Bible Training
Permanent
  Ministries
    Training
Project
  Ministries
    Training
Children's
  Training
Foreign Service
  Ministries
    Training

T.O.U.C.H.[3]
Permanent Ministries
Project Ministries
Foreign Service
  Ministries

PROPOSED ORGANIZATIONAL STRUCTURE
FOR MODEL CHURCH

---

[3] Name and symbol for the outreach ministries of the church (see p. 47). The letters T.O.U.C.H. stand for "Transforming Others Under Christ's Hand." Many who would refuse participation in an activity of a local church will not feel threatened by this new name. A large percentage of those touched for Christ will eventually share in our life as a church, but we should be willing to "give" others to other churches.

they are spending a majority of their available time in programmed church activities.

There has not been a significant change in scheduling in most churches for more than a half-century. It is time to bid farewell to a rural tradition that accommodated church schedules to farm chores.

Proposed as an integral part of the model set forth herein is the suggestion that the church meet from 9:00 a.m. to 12:00 noon on Sunday. All committee meetings would be set for 6:30 to 7:30 on Wednesday, with a fully-developed, carefully prepared worship service following at 7:30 to 8:30 p.m. An additional two-hour block of time would "float" during the week, as members find the best time for TOUCH projects.

V. *Responsibilities of Organizations*

A. *Worship*

It shall be the responsibility of the worship organization to create the services of worship for the congregation, including the use of preaching, music, drama, the ordinances, testimonies, and any features which will aid in meeting the goals of the services, including motion pictures, recordings, etc.

Today, public worship is really *private*. There is almost no free exchange of insight and conviction. Although most Christians believe in the priesthood of the believer, this doctrine does not influence their patterns of worship. Dialogue need not occur in every service, but it should take place in *some*. Other means of responding beyond "coming forward" should be provided for members in worship.

A significant distinction should be made between learning *about* God (teaching) and *meeting* Him (worship). Acts 13:2 refers to the church "ministering *to the Lord*." God craves expression of our love for who He is. Worship is a time of adoration of Him for who He is, rather than for what He has done. He desires nothing more than our love expressed in worship to Him for His total worthiness. It is the cry of the soul, deep, earnest, adoring! Here is a great and wonderful region to be explored.

Perhaps the congregation could come to understand the difference between services for worship, for proclamation, and for exhortation. Perhaps they should be announced in advance for what they are.

B. *Pastoral Care*

1. Job Description

It shall be the responsibility of the pastoral care organization to foster a true koinonia within the church, consistently and regularly visit and counsel with member families, care for members in time of crisis or distress, and initiate personal or group counseling with an individual whose conduct threatens the fellowship of the church. They shall provide leadership for personal growth retreats.

2. Organization

The active deacons shall constitute this organization.

The pastor shall be their consultant, along with other staff or nonstaff members selected by him to lend counsel or training.

They shall organize into the following leaders:

Chairman—responsible for directing the tasks and for planning. The Chairman shall represent the organization on the church council. He shall supervise the scheduling of deacons for personal growth retreats.

Family care leader—responsible for developing and directing the visitation and counseling ministry with member families.

Crisis situation leader—responsible for martialing the spiritual and/or financial resources of the church to aid those in the membership or in the community who face a period of crisis or distress; to keep intact a "prayer chain" which can be called upon for intercession for those in crisis, and to initiate any assistance possible for those involved.

43

3. The Role of Deacons

The Greek word *diakone* refers to a *servant*. Today's church has turned this word into *supervisor*. Deacons have no biblical basis for approving budgets, parking regulations, property purchases, and programs. Deacons who are relegated to such activities have been removed from a divine mandate.

Moreover, the qualifications for this Christlike activity set forth in Scripture refer to the selection of the *spiritually mature,* not the *politically secure.* Those chosen for this honor should be recognized as having unusual capacities in their prayer life; they should have previously proven capable of leading a lost person to Christ; they should be men who are visionary and creative, who expect great things from God, who hunger and thirst after righteousness, who live for Christ in all personal habits both in public and private, and who can be respected and trusted with confidences by church members. They should be "men of the Book." They should be the most spiritually committed men of the church, both before, during, and after their rotating tenure of active service.

Among others, their tasks might well include:

a. Being spiritual undershepherds of members, with six families assigned to each deacon on a rotating, annual basis. The deacon would be a "spiritual father" to these families.

b. Sharing in the worship services and ordinances. Phillip, a *deacon,* baptized the eunuch. No biblical principle would deny deacons the right to administer baptism or the Lord's Supper, and the church might well indicate its willingness to have them do so.

c. Lovingly aiding those who have deep personal need—emotional, intellectual, financial.

d. Accepting advisory supervision of personal growth retreats. Such participation in these retreats would be a key leadership role—in the precise area where a deacon should be able to inspire and instruct.

C. Personal Growth Retreats

1. Job Description

It shall be the responsibility of the personal growth retreats organization to provide weekend retreats, from Friday supper to late Sunday afternoon, for various age groups, on various topics, with different guest lecturers, offering a bimonthly retreat for each member.

Surveys of Christians indicate that their most powerful spiritual growth periods occur at retreats. The biblical example of Moses, Jesus, Paul, and others should point to the importance of this activity. In an area and era of urban pressures, such a pattern of retreat life should be a welcome oasis and an unusual opportunity for spiritual growth.

The Christian faith is not so much "taught" as it is "caught." Constant exposure in the infectious climate of a retreat should do much for the spiritual growth of the members.

In addition, the increase in Bible study or methods training, the *koinonia* developed through small-group life, the discipline of physical labor together at the retreat, the sharing in a commonly developed service of worship, should make permanent changes in the life of the church itself.

2. Physical Facilities

A retreat site of perhaps thirty acres should be procured within reasonable driving distance from the church. A modern fifty-person lodge could be erected, with twenty-five bedrooms, a chapel, a combination dining room/classroom, a nursery, and perhaps an art gallery, a library, and a craft shop. A small apartment for a semi-retired couple would be provided.

Couples attending together would have children cared for in the retreat nursery during daytime hours. Summer conferences could be conducted from June through August, replacing vacation Bible school as we now know it.

D. Training Center

1. Job Description

It shall be the responsibility of the training center organization to (1) teach the Bible to all age groups with specific purposes of evangelizing, maturing, or equipping persons for TOUCH ministries; (2) train members with the skills necessary to perform adequately in TOUCH ministries; (3) train members with the skills necessary to participate in triennial service in home or foreign mission fields; and (4) share news about the international, national, state, or local missionary activities of the denomination. Above all, it shall recognize its responsibility to equip the church primarily for ministry to others and shall place this in the forefront of all other reasons for its existence.

2. Curriculums

The matter of curriculum choice or development must be governed by the goals of the departments. They should implement the desire for all church activities to lend themselves toward helping persons relate Christ to all life situations.

The curriculum chosen should "help persons become aware of God as revealed in Jesus Christ, respond to Him in a personal commitment of faith, strive to follow Him in the full meaning of discipleship, relate effectively to His Church and its mission in the world, live in conscious recognition of the guidance and power of the Holy Spirit, and grow toward Christian maturity."[4]

"The purpose of Christian education is not simply the transmission of information, but the participation of persons in a world of 'others' where Christ is at work. Thus, Christian education helps set the stage, provides the vehicle, and stimulates the kind of activities which make it possible for a Christian to be-

---

[4] "Correlated Curriculum Design," Baptist Sunday School Board (PDP-018), p. 6.

46

come a dialogical person through whom the Word, that gives life, is spoken."[5]

It may be well for the church to offer a basic Christian library for each home in the membership. Such a selection would cost approximately ninety dollars and could be paid off in monthly installments. In addition, the church should seriously consider the initiation of a book table, to provide significant books and leaflets without profit to the members.[6]

E. *T.O.U.C.H.*

1. Definition.

The letters of the word stand for "*T*ransforming *O*thers *U*nder *C*hrist's *H*and." The symbol, a dove blending into a heart, symbolizes a Christian on mission.[7]

2. Purpose.

What should be a natural, compelling love for the unconverted has been distorted in the contemporary church. The pressure to increase income, eagerness to net gains in membership, and a concern with building sizes has made it easy to prostitute spiritual goals in favor of the pressing materialistic concerns of the institution. As a result, there is a deep-seated cynicism in the unconverted and the nonchurched. A visit from "the church" is emotionally blocked by those who are wary of being "drawn in" to another organization. Unfortunately, the

---

[5] "Basic Understanding of Program Design," Baptist Sunday School Board (unpublished paper), p. 30.

[6] See the marvelous treatise on this in *The Incendiary Fellowship* by Elton Trueblood (New York: Harper and Rowe, 1967). The basic library for the home should include a Bible encyclopedia, a Bible handbook, a Bible dictionary, a Bible commentary, a reference Bible, *The New English Bible,* and a harmony of the gospels.

[7] Symbol created by artist Erwin M. Hearne of Dallas, Texas.

Gospel of Jesus Christ is not synonymous with the word "church."

In addition, there are many who feel as did Thoreau, who said, "If I knew . . . that a man was coming to my house with the conscious design of doing me good, I should run for my life." This is precisely what the non-Christian does when someone announces he has come to visit on behalf of a church.

The purpose of TOUCH is to present Jesus Christ's love without any strings attached. If the purpose of the West Memorial Baptist Church is to share redemptively the person of Christ with unbelievers, then its concern is only secondarily to increase its own membership, budget, or buildings. If it truly believes that the *ecclesia* is the result of Christ's work in building the Church—"the Lord added to their number those He was saving" (Acts 2:47)—then its focus in outreach is toward bringing men to Jesus. Church membership is always a by-product of Christian compassion, and completely the work of the Father, not of promotion. When TOUCH is used as the instrument of outreach, those contacted will grapple first with Christ's love, not with pressures to join the church.

The TOUCH worker will be able to encourage the individual, either before or after his actual conversion experience, to participate in worship and fellowship in the organized church. Many times, this church will be that of the worker; sometimes it may be another fellowship of believers. The Father in heaven should give the direction to this decision.

This means that *all involvement with unbelievers* will be done in the name of TOUCH. Visits to the members of the church within the community would still be performed in the conventional manner, since there is no problem of bias with them.

The emblem (not the word) can be blazoned on jackets, sweaters, etc., of those who have qualified for service in this outreach ministry.

3. Job Description

It shall be the responsibility of the TOUCH organization to involve church members directly with unbelievers, so that witness with the intent of persuasion may occur in all geographical areas of the community and to the "uttermost parts of the earth," using all possible methods of involvement.

All that has gone before is simply groundwork for the members' actual evangelistic ministry, which is the focal point. Each member, having completed the basic training as a new member, would participate in one or more TOUCH missions. These missions would be people-centered, not program-centered.

This New Testament concept is almost totally absent in today's church. The church's "go" ministry is seldom, if ever, a structured one. It happens almost by accident. We should be aware that the God-given privilege of sharing Christ with others is not a permanent possession of the church. The church possesses the privilege only insofar as its members respond to it. Like the muscles of the legs, it will atrophy if it is not used.

TOUCH ministries could take place in any and all geographical areas of the community. They could occur at any and all times of the week. They might occasionally involve the corporate membership, but frequently they will involve only two or three members, often only one.

TOUCH ministries will not primarily be a means of helping mankind socially or economically, although this might occur as a by-product of the mission. They *will* point continually to the depths of human anguish and injustice, while proclaiming, "Christ is the only hope!"

Paul gave us our missionary methods in 1 Corinthians 12 and 13. He explains that the Church is the Body of Christ. It has many parts (members), each with a God-given specific function. All the members minister in *love*. Paul sees *specialization* as essential

49

to a healthy body. We have lumped nearly every one of the tasks Paul outlines into the job description of the clergyman! Each member has gifts suited to service. *Therefore, the TOUCH projects of the church will vary with the gifts of the members.*

At the beginning, two questions would have to be answered by the congregation: (1) What gifts has God given us? (2) What needs of unbelievers can we reach through our gifts, involving us in witness to them? Then a TOUCH project would be structured.

Bible study classes for various ages would be organized across the community. These would assume first priority in launching the program. However, a member gifted in painting, decorating, or even fishing would use this as a point of contact. Traveling men, involved beyond the neighborhood, would see the places they cover in their travels to be their most appropriate area of mission. Allegiance would not be to institutional programs, but to the imperatives of sharing Christ in the world. Members would, among other things, lovingly attempt to share Christ with those they meet at work and in leisure-time activities.

Public school teachers could offer courses they have wanted for years to try out, creating a center of dialogue with the unbelievers who attend. A class in interior decorating might place two Christian women in contact with twelve unbelievers. A charm course would give meaningful contact with teen-aged girls. Some men might decide to develop a TOUCH "little league" baseball group.

Research discussions will need to be conducted with doctors, lawyers, and other professional men, to explore their separate ministries to the world. The TOUCH structure would give laymen the organizational and financial basis to move from reflection to action.

Cell groups could be organized not only for Bible study, but for reaching such persons as alcoholics, drug addicts, divorcees, and outpatients who are mentally ill. The use of the small group is a potent tool in the hands of Spirit-filled witnesses.

Advertisements in the newspaper's "personal" columns would promise loving aid to those needing a friend. Perhaps a twenty-four-hour, city-wide service for those attempting suicide could be developed. Nothing is impossible! The young people might establish a coffee house. For professional men special seminars in their fields might be structured, using experts who can in their lecturing also bear witness to their faith. Other possibilities are these: work with internationals; the use of radio, television, drama, and musicals; and group therapy counseling. Perhaps a team would decide to become members of an organization like Students for a Democratic Society in an effort to reach the leaders. College students might plan a strategy for reaching delinquents who cruise the area in their Mustangs. A team of men might develop a TOUCH project of chaplaincy in the taverns and private clubs of the community. The possibilities are endless!

In each case, however, the strategy would be the same: Christians would develop friendships with five, seven, or ten unbelievers. The initial contact might center on a mutual interest in some secular area. The friendship would develop into a relationship; the unbeliever would be introduced to other Christians through a party, a Bible class, weekend retreat, etc. In time, the initial investment of love would begin to produce a steady stream of converts, to be discipled and in turn sent out to minister in the name of Jesus Christ! Christians might have three or four cycles of missions each year.

People are not the same from day to day. An unbeliever may be *closed* to the Gospel today and *open* tomorrow. Christians must be attached to them in the ebb and flow of their life. When brokenness comes, then there is openness. God reaches out to people in different ways. All He lacks in today's world

51

are the committed Christians *to be there* as a friend when He reaches.

Organizations like Royal Ambassadors, Girl's Auxiliary, etc., might be restructured just enough to make them missionary in outreach instead of being merely study groups. This is an action age; instead of reading *about* missions, our youth would be encouraged to *be on* mission.

4. Organization

TOUCH shall be under the supervision of a director, who shall be responsible for directing, staffing, and long-range planning for the organization. He shall represent the organization on the church council.

TOUCH shall divide its work into three ministries:

a. Permanent Ministries — action plans which can be recycled and continued; for example, cell groups for Bible study, chaplaincy ministry to taverns, a TOUCH basketball or baseball team. Members attached to this ministry would remain attached to it on an annually renewable basis, and assume responsibility for training incoming members in the necessary skills required.

Should a permanent ministry become large enough to warrant it, a superintendent shall be elected to give administrative attention to its needs. For example, if a combination of Bible study and baseball for boys aged eight to eleven catches on and several teams are organized, a superintendent should be elected.

Permanent ministries shall be developed as the congregation collects sufficient experience with them to feel they can be recycled for extended periods of time. It shall be the responsibility of the training center to prepare training curriculum for initial and developmental instructions for these ministries.

Report forms[3] shall be completed and submitted on a prompt and consistent basis to the director so that

---

[3] See sample of report form, Appendix A, p. 174.

the church may rejoice over results and pray for special needs.

b. Project ministries — action plans which are experimental, seasonal, or noncycling; for example, a special musical produced by the youth, or the testing of an experimental method for an agency of the denomination.

Members involved in project ministries would remain attached to them as long as they are active, and share prayer concern for those participating in other projects.

Should a project ministry obviously be effective and of such nature that it could be recycled, it shall be transferred to the list of permanent ministries. Those participating in it may, at that time, opt to be transferred with it to the permanent ministry or be reassigned to another project.

A report form for all project ministries shall be created, since the records of these activities will be source materials for establishing feasibility or reason for failure. Such records will be used to determine whether there would be any value in trying it again or under what circumstances.

All project ministries shall have a project superintendent, who shall be responsible for expenditures, reports, etc., and be available for interview by those who may be interested in the project.

c. Foreign service ministries — action plans should take members to mission fields beyond the local community which is served by the church. The word "foreign" in this context means "beyond the local community." It might involve ministering to hippies in the center of the community, conducting a vacation Bible school along the Rio Grande, participating in the life of a pioneer church in Minnesota or Utah, or sharing in the tasks of a medical dispensary in Ghana.

It shall be the objective of the church to place each member of the congregation in foreign service for a period of one to three weeks no less than once each three years. Such service shall preferably take place by groups from the church, rather than by individuals.

The following guidelines are suggested:

1) The director of TOUCH shall correspond with foreign, home, state, and associational mission boards or committees to determine areas and times when the members could make a meaningful contribution to some area.

2) He shall present the possibilities directly to the congregation, who shall decide by vote which projects shall be accepted.

3) He shall receive applications for participation from members.

4) He shall arrange for one of those making application to be appointed by the congregation as leader of the mission.

5) In cooperation with the dean of the training center, he shall arrange for either the leader or some other person, who will become the teacher of the mission group, to visit the field eighteen months in advance of the mission (six months in advance of the training).

6) The leader shall be in charge of the group while on mission. He may appoint any assistants he deems necessary to assist him in his task.

7) The director shall, in cooperation with the deacons, develop a continual chain of prayer for the mission during its execution.

8) Upon return, the mission personnel shall be provided sufficient time to share the report of their ministry with the church. They shall submit a written report to be a part of the historical records of the church, which may include photographs and tapes, and copies shall be sent to appropriate news media.

5

The Sixteen Weeks of Withdrawal

The first weeks flew by. The garage of our new home was remodeled into a church office. Equipment and office supplies were purchased. One of the members recommended her bridge-playing neighbor, Marie, for the position of church secretary. I was told Marie had been an inactive church member for many months, and I was delighted at the possibility of sharing my office life with such a person. She began to type stencils in her kitchen, preparing the new document for distribution to the membership. I was delighted to see her fully grasp *the Dream* from the very outset. She quickly equaled my own commitment to the task.

We met in a home for a midweek prayer service and used a local elementary school on Sunday. My first task was to get to know the members, and I spent every spare hour talking with each family. Gradually I began to realize that the congregation included a nucleus of people who fully understood the reasons for our new life, but, in spite of their unanimous vote, there were others who were not fully committed, who did not see the total picture. Hopefully, I felt that in time they would come to recognize the underlying reasons for our experimental framework; patience and love would work the miracle!

In my first sermon I said,

> Throughout history, the greatest movements have been born from the womb of withdrawal. Moses spent forty years apart before he was ready to lead Israel. Our Lord spent forty days in the wilderness prior to the beginning of his public ministry. Paul attended his desert seminary before becoming the apostle to the Gentiles. History is filled with examples of cities, nations, and races who became strong and creative after a time of withdrawal from other cultures.
>
> We are charged by God to become a "parable in the midst of the churches." Ours is the task of searching for the new structures God will use to reach outsiders in tomorrow's world. For us, *being* must come before *doing*. We must learn how to confess our sins, to walk together in love, to pray without ceasing. We must not begin to shape our structures until we have seen Him face to face!
>
> I would suggest we use the first four months of our life together to do something we may never be able to do again: let us declare ourselves "on withdrawal." It is not yet time to visit, to serve with activity. This is the time for us to *listen to the voice of God,* to become acquainted with each other, to understand our role, and to learn to love one another.

The sermons during the withdrawal focused upon the nature of the Church, the meaning of living the renewed life, and God's ministry for His people. Each message was preserved on tape cassettes, and members were encouraged to listen to them more than once.

When Marie finished typing the document written in Nashville, copies were bound in red vinyl notebooks, and someone named it "The Red Book." Each member was given a copy; discussion groups were appointed to study sections of it, with reports from each group to be further discussed by the entire body.

In the late fall, the congregation went to a seaside hotel for an all-church retreat. An amazing number of ninety-one attended, revealing to us the growth we

56

had already experienced while on withdrawal. In a series of dialogue sessions which stretched into the night, the objectives of The People Who Care were hammered out. Spirited discussion took place over virtually every word.

One of the first topics we dealt with was the matter of accepting people without regard for their race. Strong feelings about this topic were expressed—all on the positive side. Racists would have a hard time swimming against the current of this fellowship. Nevertheless, an amendment stating that we would "accept all men, regardless of race or color" was soundly defeated by the group. A bit taken aback, I asked the members why they had done so. With surprise over the fact that I did not understand the vote, one member answered, "Ralph, we don't intend to degrade anyone by making them think we must make a concession by singling them out for 'special treatment.' We don't wish to *write* about our open membership; *we intend to practice it!*" Thus far, we have not had a black present himself to us for membership, since we are located miles away from the integrated community. Nevertheless, we *have* accepted a former prostitute and a former burglar into our fellowship, and we will be delighted when the Lord provides some to live in our midst from any race or color other than our own.

The final list of objectives we hammered out now appears weekly on our church bulletin:

WEST MEMORIAL BAPTIST CHURCH OBJECTIVES

1. To proclaim Jesus Christ as our Lord and Saviour through worship, witness, education, example, ministry, and to honor Christ above all else.
2. To share the Christian gospel with every person in order to help him understand and know God personally as He is revealed through Jesus Christ both in the Bible and our personal experience.

3. To assist Christians and families to grow to maturity in the Christian life.
4. To be a community of Christians providing comfort, edification, acceptance, forgiveness, and strength to all with the material and spiritual resources God has placed at our disposal.
5. To develop a special concern for the youth of the community in verbal and active ways. (Tell it like it is—what Christ means to us.)
6. To extend our lives as an ecclesia (called-out people), witnessing throughout the world in accordance with the Great Commission, to places where Christians, the Christian faith and its interpretation need our assistance.

In the weeks that followed, we spent a great deal of time discussing the structural details of our new life together. During the entire withdrawal period, I had a lingering concern over the lack of spiritual maturation taking place within all members of the Body. True, there *were* unusual levels of spiritual growth occurring within many lives—but not in all of us.

I repressed my concern, however, because those who were growing spiritually were experiencing new levels of Spirit-filled commitment.

As others were growing deeper in their commitment, Gerald, our song leader, struggled with another issue: *his conversion.* Over a period of weeks, we talked privately together about the matter. Finally, this wonderful man who had shared the worship services with me for weeks presented himself as one ready to make a personal confession of faith in Christ.

The first anniversary of our little flock occurred on the first Sunday of November, 1969. One of the couples who had been a part of the fellowship from the outset, after a period of prayer, felt led to give the church a portion of their newly acquired ranch near Bellville for a retreat center. Their statement to me was "Take what you consider to be the *best* portion of our land"! Together we selected a forty-acre section bounded on two sides by paved roads.

As a part of our anniversary service, slides of the property were shown to the congregation. The offer of the gift was joyfully accepted. In addition, the half-century-old farmhouse was fixed up for immediate use as a retreat house, and another building was renovated to provide additional sleeping space, with toilet and shower added.

In less than three months, the Lord had provided what would later be named *Touch Ranch*. Now it would be possible for our future deacons to fulfill their withdrawal ministry as described in the Red Book. Never had Christians sung the Doxology with more reason to rejoice!

Late in November, we invited Dr. Charles Culpepper to be our first guest speaker.[1] This mighty man of God was the Charles Finney of China and was deeply involved in one of the greatest movements of the Holy Spirit in this century in North China. As he shared the details of how missionaries confessed personal sin, choosing God's will in the place of their own will, and of the mighty outpouring of the Holy Spirit which followed, my heart burned within me. How I longed for that level of renewal to break out among *us*.

I had preached a series of messages to prepare us for the coming of Dr. Culpepper, for I was aware that my dear flock knew little about true movements of revival. In spite of my preparation messages, his sermons were beyond the spiritual understanding of many members. In the dialogue sessions which followed, the confusion left in the minds of some was verbalized. Those whose religious history consisted only of well-modulated meetings in which nothing of unusual spiritual proportions had occurred flatly rejected his reports of revival.

---

[1] His book *The Shantung Revival* is a Christian classic! Available from your local book store or the Evangelism Division, Baptist General Convention of Texas, 306 Baptist Building, Dallas, Texas, 75201.

At that time, we were within six weeks of the end of our withdrawal. With a heavy heart, I began to realize I had expected too much too soon. We had not yet truly *touched God;* how could we touch *others?*

As shepherd of the flock, I had made an error which was to become one of God's "teachable moments" in my own pilgrimage: *spiritual growth in people cannot be programmed!* Having observed the "growth" that churches had experienced in one- and two-week "revival meetings," I felt that *four months* of withdrawal would be more than adequate to bring us all to a high spiritual commitment! I now realize how presumptuous it was to give God a time limit for what Paul taught would require a *lifetime.*

As we began to structure our organization by congregational discussions of the Red Book, controversy over nit-picking details often prolonged the meetings. Some began to ask if we *really* intended to marry our children "in a gymnasium"; others complained because they had begun to miss the traditional organizations of the church. Strong pressure was brought to bear by some to start a Sunday school class "like the one we used to have at our last church," and by the stewardship committee "to get the newcomer Baptists to join the church so our income could increase." Sadly, I began to accept the fact that our withdrawal had provided us with the mechanics of a renewed church, but many within the fellowship still had not fully grasped the basic reasons for the "experimental" character of the new church. Some even suggested we drop the use of the word. Further, not all were ready to choose God's will in every situation, regardless of the cost.

Preparations were made to constitute ourselves as a congregation on January 1—one minute after the stroke of midnight. It was our desire to be the first congregation organized in the decade of the seventies within our denomination.

After messages by our State's Executive Secretary and Dr. W. O. Thomasson from the Sunday School

Board, each member lit a candle from a common one. We then left the school cafeteria where our service of constitution was held and walked together to the nearly frosted turf outside. With candles flickering amid a circle of bodies, we committed ourselves in prayer to be "the Church in the world," to carry Christ's love to the long-ignored outsiders. It was truly a night of joy!

6

The Birth of 'Touch'

During the next six months, TOUCH became an exciting reality. Seven of our finest members joined an ex-addict named Joe Lee in ministering to long-term heroin users through a halfway house called "The Giant Step." Neighborhood Bible studies were organized, and their value was immediately felt. Another began to work with alcoholics. A care group for divorcees was added. Child Evangelism Fellowship materials were used to develop "Touch Times" for elementary school children. One couple converted their garage into a hangout for teen-agers. A "night people" ministry began, with several men frequenting local taverns wearing the new TOUCH jackets with the symbol of a heart and a dove on them.

Those who had caught the reasons for what we were doing found great satisfaction and joy in their "go-structure" ministries. From this loving outreach, faces of outsiders began to appear in our worship services. From the beginning, it was obvious to those who ministered through TOUCH that the concept was both valid and workable.

Our reputation as The People Who Care spread. Newspaper articles were written about us. One of these was an Associated Press story released across the nation, which read in part,

MINISTER SHOWS CHURCH DOESN'T NEED BUILDING

Fort Worth, Tex. — Ralph Neighbour leads a church without real estate, one that ranges from homes to night clubs seeking a pattern for the church of tomorrow.

He is pastor of West Memorial Baptist Church in Houston, the space city. For six months the church has been doing things a little differently from other Southern Baptist congregations.

"We are doing pure research," Neighbour said in an interview. He prefers not to be called "the Reverend."

"We meet in homes and schools," he said. "There isn't any real estate. It's a church like the early church—a family of God."

"We go to the bar and nightclubs," he said. "We're known by the bartender and owners. When someone comes in facing a spiritual crisis—a potential suicide, for instance— the bartender calls us. We come."

Cell Groups Formed

Such work he said "is just one of the functions for the church's cell groups. There are other cell groups for divorced men and women, children experimenting with drugs and looking for a way out, Bible study and counseling."

Neighbour recalled a recent session with a woman, 28, who he believed was on the verge of suicide. She was the mother of two. She lived with a man to whom she was not married; she was an alcoholic.

"In a situation like this," Neighbour said, "we say, 'We love you and have an answer.' It's not a denomination; it's not a religion, but a person— Jesus Christ."

TOUCH quickly began to attract people in need. A Protestant woman came to us, referred by a Catholic nun who lived twenty miles away. The nun had told the woman, "I do not know of another Protestant group who would care about helping you." People with marital problems began to require large blocks of my time for counseling.

Those within the membership who served in the TOUCH ministries found themselves near exhaustion. For me, this response from the community was a radical departure from the years I had spent in traditional pastorates, trying to figure out how to get people to "come to church." The demands upon us were so intense that there often seemed to be no time left over to sleep. Our green stickers around the community said:

TOUCH

"The people who care"
may be reached at any
time of the day or
night by calling
4 9 7 - 2 4 2 0

Many people took us literally!

At least two who were loved to Christ through those months are now with the Lord. One, a woman who went through a heartbreaking divorce, later died of natural causes. Another, a heroin addict who yielded himself to Christ at the Giant Step, died tragically when another addict with whom he was riding drove an automobile under a parked semi-trailer truck.

Billie, the radiantly lovely wife of a top executive, found her pilgrimage with Christ exploding with meaning through a neighborhood Bible study. Later her husband began to visit our worship services with her. Gradually they both grew into a new relationship with the Lord—and with us—which brought them into our membership. Recently, this brilliant man was offered the presidency of one of our nation's largest corporations. He accepted—with the stipulation that the president's office be moved from New York to Houston. We rejoice that they can continue to be a part of our life.

In contrast, another couple in our group struggled with deep rifts in their family relationships. Not willing to even consider divorce, first the wife and then the husband became transparently honest about their deep inner needs. God's marvelous healing of their lives was a joy to behold! Soon after, they were transferred to the East. How we hated to lose them. At the time, we could not fully realize that God would use them to bring renewal—and neighborhood Bible studies—to a congregation many miles from us.

Bob and Carl discovered a new kind of "fellowship" together as they shared their lives with addicts. They slept nights at the Giant Step, caring for men and women who lived in the misery of heroin withdrawal.

One of those addicts was Bonnie. Now in her late twenties, she had a nonstop history of prostitution dating back to age fourteen. For a number of years she had lived only for the needle. The world of "characters" she lived in offered her no news of Christ's love. One Sunday night Bonnie came forward in one of our worship services to accept Christ as her Lord. Still in withdrawal, she wept with joy, staining my suit coat with her thick eyeshadow.

A few days later, Bonnie began to have severe pain. As she continued to return to normal, the heroin no longer anesthetized internal physical disorders. One afternoon, she nearly bit her lip in half from the pain she had as she was rushed to a hospital. The diagnosis: disease had destroyed some of her organs, and an immediate hysterectomy was required.

Steve, one of our finest members, made all the arrangements for the operation. One big problem emerged: for Bonnie to escape postoperative pain, *addictive drugs were required!*

Bonnie made her choice: she selected the pain rather than drugs. Minimal synthetics would be her only relief.

The People Who Care stayed with her day and night for the next week. One of those nights, I dressed and drove to the hospital long after midnight, feeling that perhaps our suffering girl needed encouragement. When I arrived, I discovered eight People Who Care in her room, circling her bed with hands joined in prayer. I looked through the circle to see Bonnie, radiant with the peace of Christ upon her face, and thanked God for His power over pain!

Developing training materials for TOUCH ministries was of primary concern to me during those months. Gradually, "TOUCH Basic Training" emerged. As fully explained in another book,[1] other churches gradually began to adopt parts of our TOUCH "go structure."

A part of our TOUCH concept included encouraging members to share in a missionary project at least once every three years. An invitation from missionaries in the Orient offered opportunity for our first project to be undertaken. As a part of the All-Asia Crusade of 1970, seven members (including two teenagers) served in Hong Kong and Okinawa. These members were set apart in a special prayer meeting for their ministries prior to their departure, and in July of 1970 TOUCH foreign service ministries became a reality.

In addition, a close relationship was established with foreign students at the University of Houston. Friends from India, Africa, and Asia often visited in our services at Meadow Wood Elementary School. Many of our homes were opened to these young people who held to other world religions, and an increasing awareness of "the world beyond" developed within the membership.

The first home service ministry took some of our flock to a country church in eastern Texas where Joyce had lived as a girl. Our contribution was primarily in sharing our concepts of personal evangelism

[1] Ralph W. Neighbour, *The TOUCH of the Spirit* (Nashville: Broadman Press, 1972).

which might assist their members in "cultivative evangelism."

During the late winter months, Bill Stephens, editor of *People Magazine,* came to spend a week with us. After returning home, he wrote an article about our fellowship, which appeared in the October, 1970, issue. Bill wrote:

THE WORLD OF TOUCH

A tear made its way slowly down the lady's cheek. The counselor asked her to pray. She did, with great feeling. She prayed for a place of service, and she prayed for acceptance.

A well-to-do lady, after another service, went home and cried. She had been greeted after the service with, "I want you to know that we love you." Later, she became a member of the group.

Two heroin addicts made professions of faith. They were in their second week of withdrawal. (The national withdrawal average for heroin addicts is 2 percent.)

If I were sitting in your living room telling this story, I would gesture expansively—and speak excitedly. My voice would rise and fall with emotion. You see, I saw and felt TOUCH. That's the problem. The story is not to be listened to or read about. It is to be felt.

The feeling which later became virtually overwhelming was not particularly obvious when I first entered the Meadow Wood School in Houston.

When I boarded a plane five days later, I had a new song—and a new hope—in my heart.

TOUCH is the heartthrob of West Memorial Baptist Church of Houston, Texas.

TOUCH is a small sticker on the back of a cash register in a bar. TOUCH is a layman spending the night in a halfway house. TOUCH is a neighborhood Bible study group. TOUCH is a layman making a regular route of business establishments so as to minister to the employees. TOUCH is a woman teaching an illiterate to read. TOUCH is a family keeping an international student in the home. TOUCH is a layman coaching a little league sports team. TOUCH is a study course on Sunday morning.

TOUCH is life touching life. People becoming involved with people. TOUCH is *Transforming Others Under Christ's Hand.* And TOUCH does.

When members of West Memorial Baptist Church go out to minister they identify themselves as members of an organization called TOUCH—not as members of a particular church. They feel that they can reach persons who would normally shy away from church identification. A person ministered to must grapple with Christ's love, rather than with hangups he has about the church. When he comes into a positive relationship to Christ, the TOUCH worker may involve him in worship and fellowship. Generally, the church will be West Memorial, but not necessarily.

The people of West Memorial try to think of themselves in a New Testament sense—as a fellowship of believers. Conservative (very) in their doctrine, they believe that Jesus' commission to his people is of paramount importance. Their church structure is tailored to that accomplishment.

In beginning the TOUCH program, members of the congregation asked themselves two questions: What gifts has God given us? What needs of unbelievers can we reach through our gifts. The formula really is quite simple: The church evaluated its resources and its field of influence; then developed an outreach program to take full advantage and to make the greatest possible impact.

Ralph took me on a guided tour of several TOUCH ministries. One of the most fruitful was the first on our schedule: home Bible study groups. We visited three different groups. I was impressed with the depth of study each group—led by a woman of the church—was giving to the Bible. One group took advantage of the pastor's presence that Monday and asked him some interesting questions. The group then asked Ralph to select some appropriate commentaries and make them available for purchase. They felt the need for more guided help in their study.

As we drove to the next Bible study group, Ralph mused on the rapid progress of the people involved in the study. He was concerned about his responsibilities as pastor. "I've got to study to keep ahead," he said. "As they go deeper, so must I—both intellectually and spiritually."

"Just how does this kind of study group bring people to a conversion experience?" I asked.

In answer, Ralph described a model who attends one of the groups. She asks penetrating questions. The ladies who participate in the study come to the office and buy materials which can answer the questions such people raise. As the questions are tackled and answered, the relationship between believer and unbeliever deepens until the lost person is ready to respond with his whole life in commitment. "They are purchasing apologetic materials very heavily," Ralph continued. "They find that even though they have learned various facts since childhood, they now have to probe their own faith. Some of them are changing their ideas about various matters."

After touring the Bible study groups, Ralph drove me to Giant Step, a halfway house where drug addicts go to voluntarily withdraw. Joe Lee Kirkpatrick, an ex-addict himself, leads in the ministry.

The old rented house has been fixed up to include a chapel, an office for Joe, and other necessary facilities. Joe holds Bible study in the morning, a service at night. The whole environment is one of love. The addicts stay voluntarily, but as long as they are there, they cannot make a phone call or go out without being accompanied. Pushers park up and down the street. When an addict starts outside, they honk and wave at him, trying to sell him drugs. Weak with exhaustion, bones in his legs aching unmercifully, and sick virtually beyond description, the addict's temptation is vicious.

TOUCH ministries continue into the night. I met Ralph in his office at nine-thirty for another tour. He pointed out service stations, drive-in groceries, and other places of business which men of his church visit on a regular route. Their purpose—as members of TOUCH—is to get acquainted with the employees so as to be able to minister to them and their families.

One regular stop was an all-night doughnut shop where drugs were regularly passed. I was mistaken for a policeman because of my overcoat. Ralph wore a turtleneck sweater and a TOUCH jacket. He looked pretty straight among the hippies, but they were quite willing to discuss religion. Those we talked with had not yet been "down the road" far enough with drugs, and were not ready to make any kind of commitment.

Another TOUCH stop point was a pizza parlor—actually a beer parlor—but it was closed. Monday obviously was a slow night.

Our next stop was a bar. Ralph was trying to develop the same kind of ministry in Houston which he had carried on in Dallas. There, he had developed friendships with a number of bartenders. They called him when a customer needed help, such as the man who had lost his wife and was drinking himself into insensibility.

While some of the TOUCH ministries are sensational in their nonconformity, most of them are just Christian people witnessing in the most natural context of life. Proficiency in painting, decorating, or even fishing might be the focal point of a TOUCH ministry. A schoolteacher might teach a course experimentally. A charm course might put Christians in contact with nonbelievers. A man might coach a Little League baseball group. A doctor or lawyer might organize a discussion group to discuss the Christian morals of certain questions which interest members of his profession. Work with internationals, the use of radio and television, drama, counseling, a young people's coffee-house, inviting unbelievers to social engagements with Christians so as to include them in new relationships—all of these might be areas of TOUCH ministries.

An effective TOUCH ministry with youth takes place on Wednesday evening while adults are in Bible study. They meet for fellowship, study hall, and a period of Christian message. Youth from over the community are invited; so there are generally several unbelievers in the group. The kids make cookies, play games, sit around and talk, or study. All who come are required to attend the message.

One of the most ambitious projects of the church is the Foreign Ministry Service Training. In cooperation with the Foreign Mission Board and the Home Mission Board, an instructor will travel with the group to a specific mission field, each at his own expense. (The church has arranged financing for those who prefer it.) For six months before departure, the instructor prepares by studying about the region or country he will visit. He spends one to two weeks on the mission field, under the direction of missionaries. Upon his return to the church field, he continues his study for six more months. He then becomes an instructor, using pictures, tapes, books, objects, and interviews with missionaries, workers, and citizens of the mission field. The church's objective is to place each member in foreign service for one to three weeks at least every three years. Materials prepared by denominational agencies will be incorporated into the teaching program.

Ralph strongly pointed out that all ministries, other than visits with Baptists in the community, are carried out in the name of TOUCH. To project the TOUCH image and for identification, jackets are worn with the TOUCH symbol for members who are on assignments.

The TOUCH program is undergirded by the educational program of the church. My first introduction to this program came when I entered the auditorium of the Meadow Wood School, where the church meets. I noticed a table of books, around which several people were milling. Later, I found that the books were for sale. Ralph explained that most people like to make the books their own—mark them up and keep them for reference. Consequently, they sell books (without profit) at every service. Members buy devotional books, commentaries, Bible atlases and dictionaries, spiritual-growth books, and books which relate to studies in progress. Copies of *The New English Bible*, which is the major translation used by the church, were in abundance."[2]

The life to be lived in TOUCH demanded a spirit of faith, of commitment, and of devotion to Christ's plans. Once the program is authentically tasted, the laity can never again return to "business as usual" within the church!

[2] From *People*, October 1970. © Copyright 1970 The Sunday School Board of the Southern Baptist Convention. All rights reserved. Used by permission.

7

Some Couldn't Change

No scathing indictment is intended toward others when I confess that not all were happily committed to the TOUCH way. The initial nucleus of members included many deeply devoted Christians who had found the old, traditional patterns personally rewarding and fulfilling. Our new life-structure was not for all men.

There was also a concern expressed by some that it was "unfair to our children" to sacrifice their spiritual growth to achieve our research and development objectives. Frustration over unsolved curriculum problems surfaced from time to time. With limited membership, it was impossible even to consider "competing" with local churches who offered four-star facilities and multiple staff members for children's departments. Dismay was registered that youngsters "would grow up without concern for foreign missions" without traditional church programs which emphasized them.

Many church-oriented families who visited in our worship services were impressed by the deep spirit of love and fellowship within our group. Nevertheless, after we would spend an hour or so answering their questions about our new life-style, they would decide to join a traditional congregation nearby. One of these couples talked to me an entire evening. They later shared with me that they spent most of that night in heart-searching discussion. Their frank conclusion was that they "did not desire to be the dedicated kind of church members West Memorial needed."

In addition, we began to understand what A. B. Bruce meant when he wrote, "Ambition needs a temptation: it does not join a cause which is obscure and struggling, whose success is doubtful."[1] One man who had obviously joined the group because church membership would provide contacts for his business dropped out. Others with such motives in mind visited, never to return.

My honest relief that we were being so treated by those who had a "cultural religion" was not shared by all of our members, however. One of the key committees in the fellowship began to invite Marie to their meetings, deliberately excluding me from sharing in the decision-making process. They bemoaned our "visionary projects that were totally impractical." None of them were active in the TOUCH ministry.

Now that our retreat facility was available, the deacons were given opportunity to schedule the long-awaited "withdrawal weekends"—but in their monthly meetings a few of them deftly sidestepped the subject of scheduling them.

Further complicating the situation was the fact that the integrity of those who missed the traditional ways was impeccable! I frequently reminded myself that I had as loving and intimate a pastoral relationship with this group as I had with the members who enjoyed working in the TOUCH ministries. There was little murmuring and behind-the-scenes gossip. The situation clearly was not a problem caused by a few neurotics who would have been the dissidents in any congregation. These were wonderful, sensitive, intelli-

---

[1] *The Training of the Twelve* (Grand Rapids: Zondervan Publishing House, 1963), p. 16.

gent Christians *who could not feel at home in our new church structure!*

As a result of the integrity they showed, few within the congregation who were not in the "traditionalist" struggle knew we even had a problem. Many new members had been reached by the TOUCH ministries, and these had no Baptist heritage to cause internal conflict. I gladly accepted my role as the shepherd of *all* the members, and did not discuss the widening cleavage with any except dear, faithful Marie, my wife Ruthie, and three men who could be trusted to be impartial advisors. (One of those men later left us, but he remained a close personal friend.)

The possibility of erecting temporary buildings to serve both as a revenue-producing day care center and as a coffee-house, worship and training center, etc., met with vigorous opposition from the few, and we sadly laid the idea to rest. From the turbulence over this issue, antagonism of a personal nature developed for the first time. Some began to suggest that the time had come to invite those not in favor of new structures to join one of the many traditional congregations nearby. I could not bring myself to even consider such an action. My love for the members ran too deep to precipitate conflict.

By late April, I began to live with a secret ache in my heart. Some of it was caused by a sense of sorrow for having risked the secure future of my family on a project that seemed doomed to failure. Another part of the ache was for those who were "in over their heads" with us. On my bookshelf I had a volume entitled *The Freedom to Fail;*[2] I began to wonder if *any man* truly possessed enough courage to fail!

During my first visit with the little group who were then considering me as their pastor, I had said,

The effectiveness of our "research and develop-

---

[2] G. Don Gilmore, *The Freedom to Fail* (New Jersey: Fleming H. Revell Co., 1966).

ment center" will largely depend upon our ability to live creatively, dream dreams together, and totally yield ourselves to the Lord for direction. Many of us may not fully understand how painful it may become to "be different" from our neighbors. Although I have spent several years preparing myself for this venture, not one of us, including myself, has ever tried to live in forms of faith not a part of our past. Consequently, I make this promise to you in advance: If there comes a time when it becomes obvious that we cannot succeed in our stated purpose, I will not further complicate your lives by insisting that you continue to keep me as your pastor. I will voluntarily remove myself, to free you to pursue a more conventional shape of church life.

By mid-May I felt the time had come to free the group from their obligations to do research in renewed structures. I sent hand-written letters to friends within the denomination, asking their frank evaluation of the chances of my being considered for some other task within the denomination. Although each friend responded positively, no offers of positions ever came. I began to feel a new loneliness, caused by the awareness that many of my peers had been mystified that I would abandon my former security for a task they considered to be either impossible or unnecessary.

In July, I returned from our foreign service ministry to face once again the uncertainty of our group's future. Adding to the discouragement of these days was the fact that an anxiously awaited letter offering another place of ministry did not materialize, in spite of rumors from many sources that I was soon to be contacted.

For a week or so in August, I tried to convince myself that my best decision would be to settle down to a mammoth compromise and guide the church toward a traditional structure. I felt this would require at least a year of additional pastoring to do so, but this move on my part would make it easier for a conventionally minded minister to follow after I resigned. As the congregation existed, I doubted that they could find a man willing to come and pastor them. My heart was not in the project, however, even though I felt a sense of "oughtness" about doing it.

My own calling to be a missionary to the outsiders, however, could not be compromised! I felt more than ever that I would be leaving the will of God for my life if I gave up the thought of searching out new structures for the church. I began to prepare my sons for the coming changes we would have to face in our family life.

God's leadership, however, did not materialize. Possible plans to relate to a university where I could begin again by winning "pure pagans" to become the nucleus of a new experimental church fell through. At the same time, a polarization among the leadership at West Memorial continued to forecast a split. My commitment to my calling and my love for every single member of our fellowship could not be untangled; I could not bring myself to face the possibility of deliberately splitting our group. I felt a responsibility toward those who were unable to live in the changed structure, for they had been willing at the start to give it "a college try."

Although I tried hard to mask it, my own emotional life was fast moving through the classic symptoms of depression I had known so well, until now, only in those who came to me for counseling. I began to drag through the daily routine. Cries of "God, where are You?" came frequently in my prayer life—another new experience for me!

Encouragement was given from friends to *not* give up! Letters from pastors and denominational leaders revealed that a beginning impact was being made on other churches. After several hours of prayer and reflection, I included these lines to our members in the September Newsletter:

... We started out with a dream, and were unanimous in the vote of commitment to that dream. I do not feel the validity of the reasons for our dream have changed, *or can* change, with the passing of time. For those who are new members of the Fellowship, let me share the initial concepts of the dream:

Maybe not *everybody* should, but *somebody* must, become a guinea pig of experimentation in new methods of church life. We agreed that our fellowship would be an "experiment" in different-than-traditional methods of church life. We chose to be that guinea pig!

This was *not* to be considered an invalidation of present methods and organizations used by the church! Obviously, all of us are the product of earlier effective ministry. We are not negating our sister churches, nor are we "better" than they. Our spirit is precisely that of a *Research and Development Department* of a large industry like Westinghouse.

To search for new methodology does not mean that one is cynical about present methodology.

This decision meant these things:

a. We must have the courage to try new ideas, in the face of the knowledge that the task would be much simpler if we just used old, tested ones.

b. This means we must permit the "freedom to fail" in our projects, as well as the "freedom to succeed".... in either case, without retaliation and without bragging.

c. That *this* church has a unique task among the churches, and we cannot permit among ourselves an attitude that says our only obligation is to our own community. WMBC has a responsibility not *only* to the people of Houston, but also to thousands of other congregations across this nation who know about us.

d. That *not every* Baptist is going to feel called to join our church. A person threatened by the new—the untried—the innovative—is going to feel at unrest here. There are 200 other churches in Houston for them to select from. We cannot compromise our basic philosophy to accommodate the Traditionalist. Living in the future is more important than living in the past.

Our basic philosophy is that *this* church (*ecclesia*—called-out people) exists not to see how large it can get, nor how many buildings it can erect, but how completely it can fulfill the role of a servant-church in the community. We began with a feeling that it was something akin to spiritual outrage to pull every warm body into the membership so we might take in more money or have more "experienced" workers to fill jobs. *However,* we had no hesitation in receiving either the totally committed Christian or the weakest born again searcher after truth! The significant criteria for membership is that the incoming born again person (a) feel a Divine calling to our special task; (b) agree not to become a piece of "dead wood"—meaning that, no matter how immature his Christian life might presently be, he is on the pilgrimage of "becoming"; (c) be conscious that *this* family of God considers itself to be expendable in servanthood and willing to assume risks when necessary to achieve its goals.

We see "TOUCH" as our Ministry of Outreach, replacing well-tested, conventional, and successful outreach programs. We see TOUCH as "the tail that wags the dog" in our church, assuming that *each* member who has reached *any semblance* of spiritual maturity will be an "involved" member in TOUCH. We will be known as "The People Who Care," willing to help people who may never put a dime in our plate or even have the courage to fill our empty seats on Sunday morning.

We see the importance of forever shucking the spirit of unconcern toward each other. We realize that until we really get to know each other intimately, we cannot have any valid level of *koinonia* (fellowship) approximating God's wish for His Church. Realizing that this cannot be done in hour-long meetings, we set apart deacons to be undershepherds; to be examples before all of us of loving, concerned, involved, compassionate, Spirit-filled, pure, stewards of their own personal possessions. These men are elected with the knowledge that they will lead our members in continual retreat life; the Martins gave 40 acres and remodeled their farmhouse property so *koinonia* in retreats could begin to take place.

I know you have read the magazine article in *PEOPLE* and it pretty well tells that story about us. What it does not share is that we have gone to agonizing depths—working out curriculum problems, struggling to learn how to work in a management machinery brand new to us all, learning which members of the Team have ability and which have dependability. We have often felt that we "went dashing off madly in all directions" and have too few people for the tasks we wish to accomplish. We have been tempted to compromise to get the job done.

We have a world of fellow Christians expecting, trusting, praying, and hoping that the "Research and Development Center" will succeed in its objectives. Every single week since I came to be your pastor, we have received letters from many pastors in other denominations as well as our own—from *searching* pastors and laymen—asking us if we have anything to share yet that can help them out of the fog of tradition-bound church life that cannot relate relevantly to the society of the '70's.

We also have a sovereign God who has handed us a special candlestick and called us for a special calling and ordained us for a special work!

My prayer was that these lines would be used to call us again to evaluate our original objectives. These hopes were dashed, however, when an immediate response was a three-page letter which included these paragraphs:

In your second paragraph, you stated that "we started out with a dream." I am not sure that we as a family of God had any other dream than to build a church in West Memorial to minister to the needs of the community. I can speak for myself only, but I had and still do have a dream to develop a "spirit-filled" church, i.e., the normal Christian church, for those purposes.

. . . you talk about our church as being "experimental" in nature. In the beginning, I was in favor of the new methods we tried, but the deeper I became involved in the programs, the more justified the traditional methods became to me. It is *not* a part of my dream to become a R and D department for the Southern Baptist Convention. I cannot find any Biblical basis for this kind of church. It seems to me that we are trying to force an idea of experimentation on our church instead of spiritual growth and allow the program to naturally fall in place.

. . . you indicated that we should try new ideas. I agree, but only where we do *not* have a successful program. I get the feeling that we are prejudiced against the traditional program.

. . . you stated that our church has "a unique task among the churches." I do not believe it is so unique, as each church has the task of following God's will. Each Christian and each church has the task and it all fits into His plan.

. . . you talked about prospective members being "called" to join our church. I agree except when you continued to indicate that we cannot accommodate the Traditionalist. I am afraid that I can be considered in that category and I wonder.

. . . you state that "we shall not water down what we started out to do." I am not sure what we started out other than what I stated before. I get the feeling that what you want the congregation to do is something which I believe is not what God wants us to do. I feel that God wants to build a "normal" Christian church in West Memorial. A "spirit-filled" church is my dream, doing the Lord's will.

In conclusion, let me say that I am beginning to believe in the "traditional" methods established. In other words, what is wrong with the "traditional" church?— the methods they use or their spiritual decline? I feel like their methods are fine, but they do not have the spirit-filled membership or *koinonia* that it takes to carry out those programs. We have it and I feel we could make them work, the Lord willing.

As you can see, I feel that the entire letter to the members was a statement of your beliefs, most of which I cannot accept in my personal relationship with God, our church, and you.

I could not even begin to question the sincerity of the writer, for I realized the problem was far beyond the level of a personality clash: this was a matter of oil-and-water differences in our concepts of God's call for our lives. Sadly, I concluded that I had finally found "the courage to fail."

On the following Sunday morning, I closed the service with this statement:

To the Members of West Memorial Baptist Church:

During the time Ruth and I were considering this pastorate, we explained to the pulpit committee that we have a special task to which God has called us. This task is in the area of church renewal. To be certain the committee comprehended this, I wrote a lengthy paper for them, describing my commitments. I also outlined this in detail for the entire congregation on the day I candidated. I accepted this pulpit without knowledge of salary structure, requesting only one thing—a total commitment from the congregation to enter into an experimental church structure with me. At that time, the members were unanimous in their commitment. It was also at that time that I explained that if, after coming to the field, it became apparent we could not successfully continue in fulfilling this objective, I would not remain to complicate either the future of this church or my own special calling from God.

Since March of this year I have been made increasingly aware that it is time for me to submit my resignation. It is out of love for you and your future plans that I come to this decision. I must pursue God's primary call for my life and set you free to search out your own destiny as a church. Therefore, I submit my resignation, to take effect at once. This resignation is irrevocable and not open to negotiation.

I intend to devote this next period of my life to some measure of withdrawal to research, writing, and speaking engagements. I fondly and lovingly say "thank you" to every single one of you for your willingness to initiate this experiment with me, and I sincerely desire that the spirit of love which has marked our mutual relationship within the past year will continue to exist between us until our Lord calls us to be together with Him forever.

Our family will not remain in Houston any longer than is necessary to settle our affairs. During these brief days ahead, I do not wish for you or my family to feel any sense of embarrassment over this matter. Although we shall totally withdraw, as of now, from the life and activity of this church, our prayerful concern for your future will not cease. May God bless and keep you and make His face to shine upon you and give you peace.

8

The Dark Night of the Soul

At this point, this story must necessarily become that of the writer and not of the church. The ties were clearly severed. I avoided talking to those from the fellowship, for they did not need a specter hovering around the edges of their life.

In retrospect, it is difficult for me to piece much of October together. Indeed, it was a year before there was enough courage in my bones even to clean off the desk in my study, where correspondence and other things were allowed to remain untouched.

This chapter would be impossible for me to write were it not for my definite feeling from the Lord that other Christians may profit from understanding the depth of my discouragement and the power of God's hand. How can I describe the agony of walking in the fields at a nearby ranch, begging God to let me die, or the times driving around in my car when only my deep love for my family kept me from driving into a concrete wall? It seemed as though all the preparations of my life had led me to that moment when I would pastor our experimental church. Then it all came crashing in. There seemed to be no clear answer to my constant cry of "Why, God, why?"

At age forty-one, I was free from any commitments

of any sort. Like many a preacher, I had often "quit the ministry on Monday morning" when vexed and frustrated over church problems and neurotic people who made the ministry an unhappy situation. A couple of days spent reflecting upon the possibility of leaving the Lord's work settled once again (and forever!) the fact that I would stay in the calling of God for my life.

Toward the end of that black month of October, I also saw clearly that God's call in my life to live in tomorrow's church could not be denied. If the work could not be carried on within the setting of a local congregation, then emerging churches, ready for lesser modifications, surely could use my experience with West Memorial in the area of outreach!

That commitment permitted me for the first time to have a sense of direction from the Lord for the future. The destiny of West Memorial in my mind had *always* included the assisting of sister churches through the TOUCH ministries we were developing. Why should that stop?

I ran to get pencil and paper, and in a matter of minutes, without even so much as one revision, the nature and shape of the Evangelism Research Foundation was written:

The purposes of the Foundation shall include:

1. Research and develop valid methods of evangelism beyond those now being utilized by churches, especially relating to that portion of America's population best called "nonchurch-related."
2. Prepare and produce training aids, literature, and publications useful in equipping Christians in evangelism methodology.
3. Conduct surveys, classes, conferences, evangelistic meetings, and retreats necessary to equip Christians for outreach.
4. Provide Consultant services to Denominational agencies or organizations, enabling them to more adequately fulfill their mission in evangelism.
5. Give aid to Christians wherever located who re-

quest assistance in developing strategy, methods, training aids, conferences, evangelistic meetings, and retreats necessary to reach unbelievers in their area for Christ.

The theological position of this Foundation shall forever be that which holds to:

1. The plenary-verbal inspiration of the Scriptures.
2. The total depravity of all men everywhere apart from God's redemptive plan through Jesus Christ His Son.
3. The virgin birth, sinless life, substitutionary atoning death, and literal resurrection of Jesus Christ; and His imminent return to establish His Kingdom.
4. The personal responsibility of every Believer to utilize his total life, including time, possessions, and talent, to minister through the local church as an evangelist to the unbelievers of this generation.

Encouragement from friends came from all sides. Two men volunteered financial underwriting to make possible the necessary equipment and to meet expenses for the Foundation.

The telephone also began to ring! With a prayer of thanksgiving, I began to see my schedule fill quickly with invitations to come to churches to share the concepts of TOUCH. I had determined that I would not "circularize" this work, but would let God put together the ministries He had in mind.

In mid-November a close friend, Jack Taylor, pastor of Castle Hills First Baptist Church in San Antonio, Texas, called me to see if I could help him structure outreach ministries among his congregation. We discussed a consultant relationship for a period of one year, with his church providing a fee for beginning the TOUCH ministries, plus free office space for the Foundation. God seemed to be opening doors faster than we could enter them!

My former secretary from Dallas wrote that the work she was doing at that time would soon require her to make a change, and I felt as I read the letter that the Lord was also putting together the initial staff for the Foundation. Plans to visit San Antonio were made, and purpose for the future began to mingle with the continuing misery in my heart because of the situation at West Memorial.

My weekend visit to Castle Hills with my family included sitting in on a class Jack Taylor was teaching entitled "Dealing With the Devil." This embarrassed me! Somewhere during my seminary training I had decided that the devil was a medieval concept, more the product of Milton's pen than of divine inspiration. Out of courtesy I listened as Jack began to speak. He made the comment that in warfare there is always an enemy. Obviously, from the Scripture, it must be pretty evident to any Christian that we are in a warfare. True, our battle has been won already for us by the Christ who cried from His cross, "It is finished!"—but we are told in Ephesians 6 to stand firmly against the principalities and powers of the air. Was it not strange, said the speaker, that this generation of Christians little understood the nature of the enemy in the battle? What greater means of doing battle could there be than for the enemy to so thoroughly disguise himself that his presence was not even sensed? I left that session aware that, indeed, I had allowed *my* life to be shaped by the enemy instead of by faith.

In later months, the words of Norman Grubb were to crystallize my problem, which had existed throughout my ministry up until that point:

> Carnality is to be under the influence of the visible, tangible and temporal, instead of the invisible, intangible, eternal. We fail to bridge the gap within us between God's thoughts and God's word of faith, because we are bound by the domination of the visible. We see the blind eye, the withered arm: Christ saw the will and power of His Father to heal, and spoke the word, "Stretch forth thine arm, receive thy sight." We see the five loaves and the multitudes, and say, "What are they among so

85

many?" Christ saw His Father's invisible and unlimited supply, gave thanks for it, acted on the full assurance of it, and faith was seen to be "the giving of substance to things hoped for."[1]

It took the rest of that week, back again in Houston, for the full impact of this truth to work through my bones. I began to realize that, as a leader, I had always feared the word of man as much as I had feared the word of God! My position as a child of God gave me the right—indeed the obligation—to live beyond tangible reality and within that spiritual reality where men walk by faith and not by sight. I faced the fact clearly that my greatest problem at West Memorial had not been with outward circumstances: *it was that, as a leader, the little imp of discouragement had overpowered me again and again and again.* How stupid for a child of God to allow an unseen enemy to insert his greatest tool in the unexpected chasm of the mind and win the battle without a shot being fired!

My wife and I knelt in our bedroom on that Friday morning. I needed her to hear my prayer: for the first time in my life I claimed victory over my foe and in the name of Christ found a battle won on my knees.

Words cannot describe the joy that flooded my heart. For the first time, the whole experience I had gone through began to have some semblance of sense to it. In the process of shaping the image of Christ in me, my heavenly Father had had to take me through deep water to rinse away the froth of outward circumstances.

I called a dear friend here in Houston and another in West Texas following that prayer meeting, sharing with them the joy that was mine in having discovered the victory that comes from the application of faith to outward circumstances.

---

[1] Norman Grubb, *Touching the Invisible* (Ft. Washington, Pennsylvania: Christian Literature Crusade, 1966), pp. 18, 19.

During the three weeks preceding this, two different sources had sent me a little tract entitled "Others May, You Cannot." That afternoon as I flipped back through my unread mail, I was amazed to discover the tract, first in a hand-typed copy and then in its printed form. I read it through and nearly came apart with joy. God seemed to be speaking only to me through its message. Surely it may have meaning for someone else who reads these pages now:

OTHERS MAY, YOU CANNOT

If God has called you to be really like Jesus He will draw you into a life of crucifixion and humility, and put upon you such demands of obedience, that you will not be able to follow other people, or measure yourself by other Christians, and in many ways He will seem to let other good people do things which He will not let you do.

Other Christians and ministers who seem very religious and useful, may push themselves, pull wires, and work schemes to carry out their plans, but you cannot do it; and if you attempt it, you will meet with such failure and rebuke from the Lord as to make you sorely penitent.

Others may boast of themselves, of their work, of their success, of their writings, but the Holy Spirit will not allow you to do any such thing, and if you begin it, He will lead you into some deep mortification that will make you despise yourself and all your good works.

Others may be allowed to succeed in making money, or may have a legacy left to them, but it is likely God will keep you poor, because He wants you to have something far better than gold, namely, a helpless dependence on Him, that He may have the privilege of supplying your needs day by day out of an unseen treasury.

The Lord may let others be honored and put forward, and keep you hidden in obscurity, because He wants you to produce some choice, fragrant fruit for His coming glory, which can only be produced in the shade. He may let others be great, but keep you small. He may let others do a work for Him and get the credit of it, but He will make you work and toil on without knowing how much you are doing; and then to make your work still more precious, He may let others get the credit for the work which you have done, and thus make your reward ten times greater when Jesus comes.

The Holy Spirit will put a strict watch over you, with a jealous love, and will rebuke you for little words and feelings, or for wasting your time, which other Christians never seem distressed over. So make up your mind that God is an infinite Sovoreign, and has a right to do as He pleases with His own. He may not explain to you a thousand things which puzzle your reason in His dealings with you, but if you absolutely sell yourself to be His love slave, He will wrap you up in a jealous love, and bestow upon you many blessings which come only to those who are in the inner circle.

Settle it forever, then, that you are to deal directly with the Holy Spirit, and that He is to have the privilege of tying your tongue, or chaining your hand, or closing your eyes, in ways that He does not seem to use with others. Now when you are so possessed with the living God that you are, in your secret heart, pleased and delighted over this peculiar, personal, private, jealous guardianship and management of the Holy Spirit over your life, you will have found the vestibule of Heaven.[2]

[2] G. D. Watson, "Others May, You Cannot," (Westchester, Illinois: Good News Publishers). Reprinted by permission.

9

An Ecclesia in Agony

The fifteen weeks following my resignation were painful for me, but they were filled with an equal amount of pain for the dear congregation at West Memorial. The initial response to my resignation can be best described by comments in letters written to me by some of the members:

"I grew up in the traditional Baptist church—it was very difficult for me to change, although I realized we had to change. I really tried and was gradually accepting each and every program as they were presented, but it takes time. ... I did feel, however, that I personally failed. ... I set a high goal for myself and when I failed to obtain it (needless to say, maintain it), I was very disappointed and developed serious guilt feelings. As a result, I did less and less. ... Radical change and adjustment takes time. ..."

An outsider wrote, "Right now in my fondest memories I hear your voice softly explaining the events of being born again. Time after time I have restudied our talk. ... I chose to refuse His grace, but as the devil in me fights every day, the God in you which you shared with me grows stronger and stronger, and now I feel I must convince you that it was not you who failed me, but me who failed both you and our God.

Therefore, I tremendously feel the guilt of contributing to your decision to leave."

"In all other churches I have ever been in, the people tell you all the wrong things you do and condemn you. Our church faced people with their problems and told them how to be forgiven—and you loved them as well as God and Christ. . . . I learned what all was involved in giving my life for Christ. The Touch program helped so many people, but it changed my home too. . . . It seems like it was only a minority of the people who wanted a traditional church. I am trying to understand, but it is hard, why they don't change churches, and let the people that want the experimental church stay and have it."

As these letters indicate, a multiplicity of problems remained unsolved within the dear group. Within a week of my resignation, they voted unanimously to continue the experimental life we had started. I realized there was no real unanimity in the vote: it was a loving gesture to say, "Ralph, we love you." I knew the basic schism remained unsolved. Within a matter of days, the church had invited another man to be their new pastor, but the cleavage within the fellowship became deeper in its intensity. Less than nine weeks later, the pastor resigned. Following his resignation, another cleavage occurred between those who favored his leaving, and those who did not. Some predicted the group would dissolve entirely. The diaconate found itself caught in impossible situations, and then divided within itself. Truly, it seemed, Satan was sifting the group in an attempt to smash even the *memory* of the dream we had in the beginning.

At this time one of the members drafted a petition which read,

> We the undersigned members of West Memorial Baptist Church would like to go on record as:
> 1. Being 100% in favor of the original experimental program of this church.

2. We would like to use our signature below as a vote in favor of requesting Ralph Neighbour to return as our leader before considering any other pastor. Further, we believe that without complete unity of every individual in the church, without 100% commitment to the program and without capable leadership known to exist in Ralph Neighbour, we feel there is some serious question as to the possible success of our program.

3. We would like to vote against calling any leader as long as we are divided in our desires and plans for the church.

The reaction to the petition was one that finally divided the congregation between the traditionally committed and the experimentally committed people. Within a matter of a few days, most of those not sympathetic to the initial structure had moved to other churches. In addition, others who were sympathetic left because of tensions surrounding the resignation of the second pastor.

The invitation was then extended for our family to return to West Memorial. After a great deal of prayer and dialogue with members of the group, the invitation was accepted. God had done a work within the heart of the leader, teaching him new lessons concerning faith. He had also restructured the congregation with members basically sympathetic to the basic purpose.

The Evangelism Research Foundation was accepted by the members of the church as a part of the overall goal of not only discovering new concepts for church life, but also sharing these concepts with sister churches. The Foundation would become an integral part of the ministry of The People Who Care. Through it, I completed the commitment with the Castle Hills church to launch TOUCH ministries through their congregation. That church has demonstrated for scores of others that an effective TOUCH ministry can work within a traditionally structured congregation. Following their example, congregations in many other states, in Germany, Japan, and New Zealand have adopted the TOUCH ministries.

On Sunday, February 21, 1971, 116 people gathered for worship. The message was entitled, "But How?"

Deep scars, however, do not heal quickly. Upon my return, I recommended to the congregation that we return to a period of withdrawal, permitting the Holy Spirit time to heal hurts. I also knew that there were those remaining within our fellowship who were unsettled as to their commitment. It would not be fair to pressure them, and a few weeks were needed to allow time for them to decide whether they intended to stay with the group or withdraw from it.

My ministry during these weeks was essentially one of counseling. There were days when I could not leave the office even to eat lunch. Member after member came to share openly, and it was obvious God intended to do a very deep work within our lives. Any thought of outreach at this point was set aside. Our "journey inward" had to be finished first!

Actually, it took four months for this withdrawal to effect its purpose. During this time, family after family quietly dropped out of our work. Finally, there came a significant Sunday morning when, at the TOUCH training hour, several of the men demanded that we "get moving!" It was the sign I had been waiting for. Within a week, God began to bring new members to us.

It was about this time that I visited with a dear friend who had contributed greatly to our church through her occasional teaching and continual encouragement. She said to me, "Ralph, when a rocket leaves the earth for the moon, it requires an initial stage to get it launched. As it leaves the earth, that initial stage becomes a hindrance to its further growth. Why don't you simply accept what has happened as God's way of separating stage one from stage two, in order that you may continue to proceed toward the

goal for the church?" She was indeed a prophetess!
Stage two in West Memorial's life has been exciting
beyond description!

10

Sweet, Sweet Spirit

"There's a sweet, sweet Spirit in this place, and I know it's the Spirit of the Lord...." The launching of the TOUCH ministries was accented by the first annual TOUCH Day Camp, held at TOUCH Ranch. Approximately fifty children, most of them from outsider homes, participated in this ministry. The congregation purchased a bus to transport them to the ranch. Deacon's retreats were launched. The church office, which almost from the beginning had been located in an apartment complex, moved to a larger apartment. A former Houston Oiler football player was baptized into our fellowship. Other families began to share in our membership and our ministry.

By summer, the building committee had worked out an arrangement with a local day care corporation for our first building. The agreement called for us to pay off 36,000 square feet of the 100,000 square feet of property we had acquired next door to a football stadium. In return, the day care corporation would build a 10,000-square-foot, carpeted, air-conditioned structure on our land. For twenty-five years, The People Who Care would receive rent-free use of this facility during evenings and weekends; it would be used for day care until 6:00 p.m. each weekday. This would provide worship and Bible study space for us, without heavy expenditure for real estate. The entire amount the church would save under this arrangement over a quarter of a century would be approximately $283,000. The congregation enthusiastically accepted the proposal. It quickly swept through all committees, and in a period of one week $36,000 had been raised to pay off the land. Member families dipped into savings accounts, sold stocks and bonds, and obtained personal loans from their banks to secure the necessary funds to make this possible! One cannot adequately write about the excitement within the fellowship during this period.

The messages and teaching sessions of the congregation were widely sought after by individuals and other congregations. As a result, the *TOUCH Tapes* ministry was born, and one of our members borrowed a large sum to purchase the necessary commercial equipment to reproduce cassettes, providing instructional aids and inspirational truths to those within and beyond the congregation.

A "Jesus Rally" attracted over two hundred young people from the community. The TOUCH ministries began to expand, including Bible study groups, a ministry to parents of retarded children, and the use of an apartment house clubroom for "H.O.P.E." (Helping Others Practice English), a ministry to oriental women who were learning to speak and write English. As the weeks sped by, the training program of the congregation began to be structured around a newly-printed forty-eight-page *TOUCH Basic Training* manual.

A number of the members went to Richmond, Virginia, to assist the Hatcher Memorial Baptist Church in beginning TOUCH ministries. This began with a weekend of lay renewal testimonies, followed by two weeks of intensive instruction. The first week was devoted to a "journey inward" in which the Hatcher Memorial members were encouraged to understand the meaning of the Spirit-filled life. The last week dealt with the practical matters of TOUCH ministries. The result was over one hundred twenty people trained, thirteen men for a bar ministry, forty-two teenagers for rap sessions, four weekday Bible studies, and three children's activity times.

A group from Uvalde, Texas, came to share in our life. Dr. David Haney, pastor of the Heritage Baptist Church in Annapolis, Maryland, contributed a manuscript entitled *Renew My Church* to the work of the Evangelism Research Foundation, and Dr. Elton Trueblood graciously wrote a foreword to it.[1] The manuscript for *The TOUCH of the Spirit* was completed.[2]

In the fall, the TOUCH ministries scheduled a "TOUCH Fair" with eleven different ministries presenting their outreach in booths set up around the room. Another TOUCH ministry was born when two nurses within the church saw an opportunity to relate to outsiders by giving allergy shots to those within the community.

The use of our new building gave a feeling of stability to the group that we had not known previously. However, the congregation did not change its basic commitment to minister beyond church walls, and the weekly record of ministries indicates that since moving into this facility for public worship, we have more than doubled the use of other facilities within the community for outreach.

Before the end of the year the Lord had also made it possible for the group to have a weekly television broadcast. Entitled "The Touch Family," the thirty-minute color program featured two Christian clowns (Giggles and Touchey), the story of a child in pain, testimonies from members of the church and other Christian friends, the sacred music of Ron and

---

[1] David P. Haney, *Renew My Church* (Grand Rapids, Michigan: Zondervan Publishing House, 1972).

[2] Ralph W. Neighbour, *The TOUCH of the Spirit* (Nashville, Tennessee: Broadman Press, 1972).

Patricia Owens, and messages which range from being evangelistic to dealing with the role of laity as ministers. Response to the telecasts from the greater Houston area has been more than was expected.

It also became possible to add an associate pastor to the staff of the congregation. After a number of men who had been professionally trained were interviewed, God clearly led the congregation to invite Harold Tate, a man who had taught mathematics in a high school for nineteen years, to fill this position. (It seemed only logical for a church committed to the ministry of the laity to invite one from among the laity to serve as a shepherd.) Their choice has been one obviously directed by the Holy Spirit!

The Foreign Mission Board of the Southern Baptist Convention recognized the significance of our ministry in December of 1971 by inviting the pastor to spend a month in Asia sharing the concepts with missionaries. State Baptist conventions have extended invitations for the life style of The People Who Care to be explained to pastors and laity across their states. Groups of pastors have continually extended invitations for news about the go structures to be shared. Pastors from Japan and New Zealand have come to spend time observing the work.

The concept of withdrawal was experienced again in the late winter of 1972, when the first annual Evangelism Research Foundation Swiss Seminar was held in Chateau d'Oex, Switzerland. Capacity enrollment from America was joined by missionaries from Europe who came together to experience the "journey inward" and the "journey outward."

A ten-acre lake has been partially completed at TOUCH Ranch, and the dream of its completion, with lovely facilities surrounding it in the heart of the Texas hill country, will one day become a reality. In less than one year the congregation has outgrown the day care center and plans to erect a multi-functional building to be used, as one member humorously commented, "eight days a week." The space utilized for worship will be so designed that it will also be used for a dinner theatre, a coffee house, a roller skating rink, a gymnasium, a cafeteria, Bible study, and day care.

Seminars explaining the concept of West Memorial and the TOUCH ministries are held in various parts of the nation. It hardly seems possible that, in such a short space of time, God could use a fellowship, which numbers two hundred people at this writing, to accomplish so much!

Perhaps the best way to conclude the beginning of the story of The People Who Care would be to quote the statement made in the bulletin printed for the dedication of the day-care building:

> West Memorial Baptist Church, for the past three years, has been a house church. We have functioned with the conviction that God has created us for Himself, and that all we possess is His before it is ours. We continue to minister through our homes each week, utilizing them for Weekday Bible Studies, TOUCH Times for kids, etc. We believe firmly that the church referred to in the New Testament is comprised only of people, and that church buildings should be used for more than a few hours of religious activity each week.
>
> Our role has been described by Dr. Kenneth Chafin, Secretary for Evangelism for our denomination, as that of "a parable in the midst of the churches." Our discipline in membership, our concept of stewardship, our intermember relationships, are all based upon the conviction that we are the body of Christ, and that we exist only to reveal Him.
>
> Our membership is not comprised of "super Christians." Our family includes fragile young Christians searching for truth and those who have only recently come to know Christ. We have accepted as our definition of evangelism, "One hungry beggar telling another hungry beggar where to find bread."
>
> Perhaps no other church should even consider copying our life style, but we do feel individual elements of what we have done could revolutionize

traditional church structures. For this reason, our concept of the use of buildings and our ministry through the organization called TOUCH have been readied for dissemination to other churches. We encourage others to consider the possibility of including a ministry which would function entirely beyond the church walls and we would be delighted to lend assistance from our own experience to such groups.

PART TWO

A LOOK AT CHURCH RENEWAL

11

How a Seven-Year-Old Boy Learned About Renewal

Having been born in the kitchen of a parsonage has some advantages. Among others, one gets in on all the dirt about the church members at the dinner table (and is threatened with an extra thousand years in Purgatory if he ever opens his youthful mouth!). As a result, this preacher's kid grew up with the awareness that not all was sweetness and light among the children of the King.

The very real Person of Christ invaded me with His presence at the very early age of five, as Dad knelt with me in his study beside an old, creaking rocking chair. His wonderful life living within me made me certain that this church thing had some validity in it *somewhere*. If it had not been for my own invasion by Him, I might have revolted against the whole situation and become the world's greatest pagan.

Something happened to destroy that attitude forever when I was seven. The church Dad pastored was, I am sure, far more spiritual than most—but it had its problems. There were those within who hated each other, who were jealous of each other, who demonstrated unspeakable selfishness; and they often kept Dad on his knees. His preaching illuminated my mind, but his praying kept me aware that God had a work to do in our church.

Albert Peterson, evangelist, came to conduct a two-week meeting for us. I sat on the very front row (where I could be watched by Pop!) and did not hear very much of the minister's message. I was too young to understand it, but that man communicated nonverbally with me in an amazing way. He simply glowed with the presence of Christ. He, along with many others in our fellowship, really did live under the ownership and operation of the Master.

I guess that the services were typical of most in effectively reaching sinners, but the final Sunday night is when everything broke loose. During the invitation, some of God's children saw their need to be more fully redeemed from the power of sin in their lives. One by one, there was confession of the things I knew all too well had existed in our group. There was neck-hugging, some folks kneeling together in prayer for the first time in their lives, some genuine repentance.

That night the service lasted far beyond my bedtime, and when we finally returned to the parsonage, I could not sleep. God had truly revealed His power in that church auditorium! What began that night, furthermore, continued in the days ahead. Although Rev. Peterson left on the train the next morning, the deacons requested Dad to continue the services, preaching himself. It was the beginning of a mighty movement of God in that community.

Days stretched into weeks. The eventual termination of night services did not end the Presence in our midst. Our county sheriff was converted and subsequently volunteered to the governor his confession of illegal activity. Tried and sentenced, he went to serve his time rejoicing in the Master's forgiveness. He later returned to influence scores of others by his testimony.

A minister of a "modernist" congregation in our community was caught up by the renewing Spirit within God's people, and he came to observe our services. Later, he confessed to Dad, "I have not got what that Bible is talking about! I have not been born again." His personal experience with the living Lord not only altered his ministry (and his address!), but also touched *this* little fellow with the awareness that God *could really change the world* when He was free to walk unhindered among His children!

The memories of the long ago are somewhat clouded as to all the details, but the impact of that weeks-long movement of God in our midst spoiled me forever for the tedium of grinding out church activity in fleshly strength. In the passing of the years, I have often looked at the problems of the church from the viewpoint of an adult and have longed to be a boy sitting on the front pew once again, watching the people of God become alive with brokenness, love, zeal, and compassion.

That experience, called by some "revival," was also "renewal." In that period of church history the word had not been coined for church use, but it *happened* as the result of renewed lives in God's family. Bible classes came to surprising life; the men of the church began to enter the taverns of that town to share the Good News; men in business cleaned up shady deals; worship services were vital, redemptive. A church became the Church, the Body of Christ.

What happens to the church when a generation or two drifts by without experiencing the power of God moving in its midst? The answer to that question, as the song says, is "in the wind." Look around! It goes through the motions. It lives without creative leadership from men who follow after the Spirit's direction. It relies on old forms that were "good enough for father, and good enough for me." It clings to old structures that formerly were filled with the Spirit, unaware that God does not live in buildings, programs, literature, or anything else made by human hands. It doggedly believes that in those old structures of church life which proved to be so vital in sharing the Gospel in yesterday's world, there is some mysterious ingredient which will certainly recycle into life if we just wait long enough.

Or, it may fill its lack of fire with wildfire, replacing the breath of the Spirit with the wind of emotional fanaticism. Again, it may suggest that God is dead and powerless in this secular age; some churchmen blame a failing dynamo for their condition!

Still another possibility: church leaders may decide that what they need to do is become "relevant" to the present culture. Aware that the old forms are not adequate for today's world, they may enter into careful studies of the sociological and psychological structure of our culture. They may study the philosophy of mass communication, the gimmicks and programs that seem to be attractive to the modern man. They endlessly propose "the solutions," which turn out to have little more power in them than that which was required by their originator to tap his pencil on the desk while trying to come up with them.

How can a man who does not know how to communicate in an intimate and personal way with the Lord of the Church ever expect to find the solution to its problems? Renewal does not begin with structures, nor with programs. It begins with true penitence—sincere confession of the sins of pride and willfulness.

Joshua was spending a particularly restless night prior to the time he was to lead the children of Israel into the promised land. As he agonized over his plans, the angel of God appeared to him. Said Joshua, "Are you on *our* side, or will you be on the side of the enemy in the coming battle?" Replied the angel, "Joshua, I'm not on *either* side! I am with the Lord Jehovah: now, Joshua, the question is, are *you* with Him? If you are, follow me!" (Joshua 5:13-15).

Renewal in the church of this age will authentically occur when we, with Joshua, learn to *listen to God* before we even begin to think about the strategy or structure required to fight on His side.

Countless renewal groups havè developed within the land. They live inside and outside church walls, with and without budgets, clergymen, programs, committees, or formal services. The disillusioning thing about practically all of them is the fact that they have the same basic "people problems" that the institutional churches have. People who are carnal in the old structure are going to be just as carnal in the renewed structure! What God's children need first of all is a renewing of their lives to be made conformable to His will and His direction. Unless and until that happens, the newly devised forms are going to be as powerless as the old.

We are creatures of impatience. The answer for which we struggle will not surface overnight. It will come as the result of heart-searching prayer and agony of soul.

Ian Murray writes of the manner in which young Spurgeon came to his ministry at New Park Street with these words:

> Spurgeon came to London conscious that God had been hiding His face from His people. His knowledge of the Bible and of Church history convinced him that, compared with what the Church had a warrant to expect, the Spirit of God was in great measure withdrawn, and if God continued to withhold His face, he declared to his people, nothing could be done to extend His kingdom. It is not your knowledge, nor your talent, nor your zeal, he would say, that can perform God's work. "Yet, brethren, this can be done—*we will cry to the Lord until He reveals His face again.* All we want is the Spirit of God. Dear Christian friends, go home and pray for it; give yourselves no rest till God reveals Himself; do not tarry where you are, do not be content to go on in your everlasting jog-trot as you have done; do not be content with the mere round of formalities. Awake, O Zion; awake, awake, awake!"

To the end of his life Spurgeon pointed back to

the revival at New Park Street as one sure evidence that God answers prayer, and he would often remind his congregation of those early days. "What prayer meetings we have had! Shall we ever forget Park Street, those prayer meetings, when I felt compelled to let you go without a word from my lips, because the Spirit of God was so awfully present that we felt bowed to the dust.... And what listening there was at Park Street, where we scarcely had air enough to breathe! The Holy Spirit came down like showers which saturate the soil till the clods are ready for the breaking; and then it was not long before we heard on the right and on the left the cry, 'What must we do to be saved?' "[1]

God-sent renewal will not occur within the church of this generation until we begin to confess that without the leadership of the Holy Spirit nothing at all *can* be done! The problem, then, is twofold: first, there are those who are not willing to wait for the Spirit's solution to our present dilemma and who would lead us into self-devised, carnal solutions which are not God-breathed. On the other hand, there is the painful problem faced by some men who are genuinely Spirit-led in proposing roads to renewal, who find themselves summarily rejected by Christians who do not wish to pay the price required to become an authentic expression of the Body of Christ in this age. Only a sovereign God can lead us out of our dilemma!

[1] Murray, Ian H., *The Forgotten Spurgeon* (London: The Banner of Truth Trust, 1966), pp. 42, 43.

12

The Yesterdays That Light Us to Dusty Death

God created man to venerate the past, and that is a valuable quality. Like many other couples, my wife and I enjoy the antiques that are included among our home furnishings. They remind us of our forefathers and of a golden age when charm, dignity, and un-pressured living were in evidence. Our antiques, how-ever, are not in the kitchen. In that work area, where efficiency is "absolutely necessary" for survival, the most modern and up-to-date methods of cooking, cool-ing, and cleaning are not considered luxuries.

To recall our past, to venerate our heritage, is a vital part of the activity of the living church; *but the church must keep its assemblage of antiques out of the "kitchen."* When the work of evangelism, teaching, and ministering are done, we need modern tools for modern men. Those contemporaries whom we lose to the devil by trying to reach them with our antique kitchen equipment are *least prepared to die!*

Most of the antiques we have carried into the last third of the twentieth century belong to the nineteenth. That century was, indeed, a creative one. It gave to Christendom the pattern of modern missions, launched by William Carey in 1795. Charles Grandison Finney, living in its first half, saw revival sweep the Northeast;

Dwight Lyman Moody saw crusades move England and America to Christ in the last half. Charles Haddon Spurgeon was used of God to raise up one of the first numerically large nonconformist congregations; they not only worshiped, but also cared for orphans and trained ministers to evangelize through "Bible School." England continued to feel the power of Spirit-filled Methodism which was propelled into that era by John Wesley's work in the late 1700's. It was the golden age of knowledge, when the amassing of information into Bible dictionaries, commentaries, and encyclopedias occurred at a rate unequaled before or since. Robert Raikes fathered the modern Sunday school movement just in time for its development within the century; he was propelled by William Fox of Clapton, England, a Baptist layman, who organized the first Sunday school society in London.

Sometimes one feels that the present century of Christians can be likened to the son of a great genius. Born in the shadow of his father's greatness, he strives to equal him, but becomes content to rewalk his father's footsteps rather than to blaze new trails.

Consider one simple example of how this century of Christianity has, up to now, done just that. I refer to the established time for worship on Sunday morning: 11:00 A.M. Can you name any other event of contemporary life that takes place at this odd hour? Schools, businesses, offices, agencies of all sorts begin their day at 7:00, at 8:00, or 9:00. Only the church continues to begin its Sunday school at 9:45, with worship at 11:00. Why? There is an antique in the kitchen!

During the golden century, men and women lived in a rural society. Small villages dotted the countryside, with people scattered between them on farms. Papa had to get up at daylight on Sunday to water and feed animals, collect eggs, and perform other necessary chores before the homestead could be vacated to attend church services. Mother heated her water in a kettle, poured it into a wooden tub, and while the children bathed in it, she took her iron from the top of the stove and pressed shirts and coats. After the horse was rounded up and hitched to the buckboard, the family rode down the mud-rutted road to church.

Eleven o'clock was an accommodating hour for those who had to put in a half-day's work before arriving to worship! Contrast that with today's culture: While Mother cooks bacon and eggs on a table-top stove, the family can prepare to evacuate their suburban home or apartment in a flat thirty minutes. Shirts are wash-and-wear, laundered in automatic washers and dryers. The shiny family auto speeds the clan to the church building on expressways. *Yet we still arrive at the hour set by our great-great-great-grandfathers!* Why?

Some months ago, I endeavored to trace the history of the Sunday evening worship service. Still a vital part of evangelical church life, it has completely changed audiences during the past thirty-five years. When I was a boy, our church bulletin advertised the "Sunday Evening Evangelistic Service." It *was* an evangelistic service. Music, sermon, invitation, all were geared to the proclamation of the Gospel to unbelievers in a packed auditorium. Moreover, when the invitation was concluded, more often than not many people went away converted. Many more left the auditorium under deep conviction, to return the following Sunday evening to make public their decision to follow Christ.

Today, you can fire a shotgun four ways in a Sunday night service, and you will be extremely fortunate to wound even *one sinner!* There are exceptions to this in occasional churches, but they are only the exceptions that prove the rule. Churches still attracting large crowds on Sunday night in my denomination are doing so by a high-powered organizational program which requires many people to come out to sing in choirs, teach pre-service classes, or fill other

111

elected jobs. They, along with their families and friends, comprise 99% of the audience. Even then, in 95% of churches still sponsoring evening services, the size of the crowd will be from 30 to 50% of the Sunday morning attendance. More significant, the minister these days usually preaches his evangelistic sermon in the *morning* service and *teaches Christians* on Sunday evening. The bulletin seldom advertises the evening service nowadays as "evangelistic."

Have you ever wondered why evening services were initiated in church life? What was the motive for beginning them? Two days of research in a library were required to write this next paragraph.

In the early part of the nineteenth century, evangelical ministers were quite sensitive to the need to evangelize the last man, woman, boy, and girl in their community. They used any available device as a point of contact with unbelievers. In 1792, William Murdock developed the coal-gas light in England. From that date until about 1823, artificial illumination was made possible in London, and gas was piped to factories, stores, and public places. Because gas lights were still too expensive to be installed in homes, people flocked to buildings where this new invention made the room "as bright as day." Enterprising ministers were quick to take advantage of the "fad" and installed gas lights in the sanctuaries. They initiated Sunday evening services, attracting large audiences who were not interested in religion *per se* and who did not attend morning services.

The motive for initiating the first Sunday evening services was evangelism! They used the fad of the gas light, along with human curiosity, to proclaim the redemptive message to people unreachable through other means.

Evening services continued to be evangelistic in tone through the rest of the century. As curiosity about gas lights waned, enterprising ministers of that age discovered still another need of the unbeliever which would

112

attract him on Sunday night. The night service became the gathering-place for singing, special music, gaiety, and informal fellowship. Sermons were dramatic, filled with heart-rending illustrations. In an era bereft of entertainment, the service filled a need for it and continued to win the otherwise unwinnable.

We still have the antique service scheduled in our Sunday bulletins, but it is no longer an effective tool for evangelism. Moderns are choked and gorged by professional entertainment on color television sets. In our pressured lifestyle, the last thing the family needs is an unnecessary service to attend, another night required to "go out." The relic is still supported by the faithful few, but it is a poor device for the proclamation of the Gospel in our day!

Businessmen often fly to distant cities on Sunday evening so they will be fresh for Monday conferences; weekenders fill the highways with unbelievable traffic jams as they return home from the beach or the mountains on Sunday nights. The most succulent fare from Hollywood is dished up on television. Why do we not seek a *new* and *contemporary* reason for Sunday evening services through which men and women can be evangelized? If this is not possible, would it not be wiser to "give back" this block of time to committed Christians and ask them for the same time-investment at another period of the week when they may become effectively involved in outreach?

A few years ago, I watched a church in Paoli, Pennsylvania, disburse its members through cell groups for evangelistic Bible study on Sunday evenings. The pastor kept the night worship service intact with a handful of members who lived near the church, but many families who lived considerable distances away began Bible studies in their homes. Neighbors were invited to attend. The response was superb, and many unbelievers were reached for Christ. In a church with one hundred and fifty members, as many as sixty to seventy unbelievers were being reached on Sunday evenings through this method. Robert Couch, then pastor of the church, was hard pressed to keep up with the training of all the new Christians harvested from these groups.

One wonders if it is time for evangelicals to put away their sentiment for the antique service which originated with the gas light and to get on with the business of *reaching people!* Is the main concern of the church to "meet," or is it to get involved redemptively with unbelievers?

13

Evangelism Methods — the Same Yesterday, Today; Will It Go On Forever?

Most of the golden age evangelistic methods were creative and innovative; in short, they truly belonged to that century. Those men of God were anxious to reach their generation for Christ, and they set magnificent examples of adjusting the theology of the cross to the sociology of their time, developing techniques which truly reached unbelievers.

Consider the religious climate of that day: theirs was a God-oriented age, when the occasional atheist in the village stood out like a sore thumb. Almost everyone *believed* in God, whether they were willing to be His true followers or not. The Bible had not yet been attacked by Wellhausen's higher criticism (this did not begin until 1880), and it was readily accepted by most people as the authoritative Word of God.

Moreover, the minister often ranked first in prestige within the community. He was usually an educated man among the uneducated, called on not only to teach and preach, but also to give advice to unschooled members concerning financial and even legal questions. "Elmer Gantry" had not been written, nor had the Protestant church been "used" for personal profit by entrepreneurs.

Churches in that day were not competing with each other for members and dollars. Sheep-stealing was not a problem; shepherds were too busy tending their flocks. The church did not have to prove it was successful. It was enough to be found faithful by the Master.

"Modernism" reared its ugly head late in the century, but until the end, the climate for evangelism was one which could presuppose that sinners basically *believed* in heaven, hell, the resurrection of Christ, and His virgin birth. Preaching and methodology reflected this.

Consider also the social climate of that day: there were few outlets for entertainment or diversion. People did not travel far; news was not yet carried with the speed of light. The family was an integral unit, and people usually spent many evenings at home, uninterrupted by P.T.A.'s, clubs, political meetings, etc. "Going out" was an event.

Theirs was a day when a man was a man, not a Social Security number. He was known and understood by far more of his fellowmen than he is in our age. As a result, he had far more of a sense of personal identity and responsibility than his counterpart in this last half of the twentieth century.

God's men in that culture found a vehicle which was truly God-sent. Called a "revival" in the South, "evangelistic services" in the North, country towns and cities, too, were invaded by weeks of great preaching and singing. A "brush arbor," a tent, or even a wooden tabernacle was erected, usually following the harvesting of the crops. It was a festival period which often surpassed the circus and the traveling theatrical group in attracting crowds. Methodists, Baptists, Presbyterians, all, came; it made no difference what one's denomination was, for these services were the social gathering places for all people in the area. With no radios, gramophones, or other forms of entertainment, these meetings were both "social" *and* religious. People were content to listen to the marvelous singing of the quartet or soloist, the accomplished playing of a specially-important pianist, and the colorful preaching of a minister who often had developed his own ability as a showman as well as a Bible expositor. Sam Jones could have his spittoon beside the pulpit; it simply added to the colorful man's exposition of the Gospel.

Here were men of God (for the most part) who were anxious to win all men by all means. This "revival" meeting was not a part of the long-term history of the church; it rooted basically in the pattern of Whitefield, set a few generations before. *But it reached people!* And through it many thousands were converted. The frequently poorly-educated listener of the audience never thought about mentally debating the message of a man who was much more learned; "one-way" preaching was acceptable. The minister who stood to defend the Bible against the town atheist was, in essence, often using a device which would give him a sympathetic hearing from many a sinner who was horrified at atheism.

These meetings were often "protracted," a word meaning that they went on for many weeks. One description of them indicated that the minister would preach a solid hour each evening for the first two or three weeks, teaching the Bible principles of salvation and sanctification to the audience. Then, for another week, he would preach forty-minute messages which were directed at backsliding church members. One report of this period suggests that people would leave each night deeply distressed over their own lack of concern for the lost, their selfish patterns of life, and unconfessed sins. Invitations following the sermons did not begin in the protracted meeting until people began to *insist* that they were needed, perhaps three weeks after the services had started. By this time, the mind and the emotions had been touched by the messages, and decisions were deep and long-lasting. Then the minister's messages would be reduced to twenty minutes in length and would usually be a loving, gentle appeal to follow Christ; the invitation could easily consume forty-five minutes to an hour. The meeting would then continue for as many days—or weeks—as the "spirit of revival remained" in the town.

In the passing of days, the revival meetings and protracted meetings were less and less effective in reaching sinners. Theater, cinema, radio, phonographs, increased transportation methods, and enlarged educational facilities all contributed to changing the American culture. People no longer met in masses following harvests. The social climate changed. Life became pressured. Skepticism leaked into the college set from professors who openly challenged the very roots of Christendom.

The effectiveness of the meetings waned, and so did their length. People no longer lived such unpressured lives, and the meetings were shortened from six weeks or longer to three weeks, then two weeks, then to the current schedule of one-week meetings. Often nowadays churches schedule weekend emphases.

Large groups of unchurched are never reached by today's "revival" meeting. They are warned that a revival meeting is coming to the local church on the corner by large placards advertising "REVIVAL!" and portraying "mug shots" of a preacher and a singer, and they decide to stay away—by the thousands!

Married to the method which was so effective in another age, the church leaders were hesitant to give it up. The creative capacity of our forefathers far and away exceeded anything we have known thus far in evangelism today, and we have not shown the same capacity to innovate in this entire century in a manner equalling that included in our inheritance.

In order to preserve the "action" of these meetings, all sorts of gimmicks were added: "pack-the-pew plans," special services during the Sunday school hour for children aged eight to twelve, in which pressure was often placed upon youngsters to "come forward and be saved." Many came forward and were reported in the magnificent "harvests" of sinners. More and more, the services were attended by members of the church. New phrases were born, such as the "inside census" (which should have betrayed to all what was happening!) in which lists were made of members' relatives not yet converted and those who attended the church services who were as yet not members. Extensive visitation to these people produced results worth reporting to the other ministers of the area—but no one mentioned that these were, indeed, "church-oriented" people who were being converted by the meetings. A blind spot had appeared among many ministers. They were not willing to admit that they were preaching to the segment of the community still church-oriented and God-oriented. Quietly, large masses of the American population had tiptoed over to the non-church-oriented, skeptical, cynical side; for a long time it seemed that the church did not even know what had happened.

Ministers in evangelical churches today are confused about what they should do with the revival meeting. Should it be directed to sinners who are not present, using evangelistic messages which are quite simplistic to an audience usually comprised of the most faithful members of the church? Or should the emphasis be on a "deeper life" message to help Christians grow? Can both emphases possibly be combined in one short week of time? Most people who are truly faithful to the services are not able to attend more than 70% of them, due to the competition of secular responsibilities. Unlike "yesterday," the revival meeting is in trouble with competition nearly every night of the week and every week of the year. P.T.A., band practice, little league practice, athletic competition at the local high school, homework, garden clubs, civic clubs, women working days, men out of town for the week on business—the list of reasons may well be endless!

In our world, the family of God has a real struggle to get together on a regular basis to do something as a congregation during the week. For them to be involved in any significant amounts of involvement with unbelievers during the week, in addition to attending the services and singing in the choir, requires superhuman energy.

This writer wants to state vigorously and vehemently that he does *not* feel it is time to do away with the revival meeting. It is almost the only thing done in most evangelical churches in this generation which still concentrates on the reaching of unbelievers. To simply abolish it because it is "outdated and outmoded" would be a colossal disaster! Many church-oriented people can still be reached by these services, and surveys I have taken in scores of churches indicate that the great percentage of their present faithful church members were reached for Christ and made their decision during a revival meeting. This points up the fact that it is just about the *only* thing of worth we have been doing to reach unbelievers. It does *not* reveal the huge vacuum we have left in evangelism by limiting ourselves to revivals as the major method of outreach of the church.

Many, many areas of our nation still remain where the society is comparatively unhurried and still quite rural in context. In these areas, revivals are far more effective than in the cosmopolitan cities, and they may well be vital in reaching unchurched people for another full generation. City-wide meetings continue to be an excellent cooperative way for the Gospel to be communicated to the unchurched, especially when the stadium meeting can be televised live to hundreds of homes in the area.

Many ministers have realized that the basic non-religious reason for unbelievers attending revival meetings has always been for entertainment. They are alert to what can happen by inviting an unusual speaker who has achieved some secular notoriety—like a pro football player, a former movie star, a well-known recording artist, etc. This awareness has resulted in bringing in large crowds to services. Although such crowds are usually composed of Christians from sister churches, whenever there is motion, some unbelievers are going to be swept into the services and a few converted.

Occasionally in our generation we have been given God-led men who not only have the ability to communicate the Gospel effectively, but who have also developed the ability to entertain. Evangelists who include folk singers in their meetings and who know the problems of today's teen-agers reach out to thousands of young people unreachable through routine meetings. Men who are colorful, courageous, and truly sincere in their ministry should be honored guests in the churches of this generation. They have enough sense to realize that men have never enjoyed reading a poorly printed magazine or watching a black and white film when they could see it in full color. They have developed their talents and skills in order to reach men otherwise unreachable. God bless 'em— and a bushel of onions to the prudes who think they are too flamboyant or too "fleshly." Sam Jones went down in history as a great soul-winner—and what could have been more fleshly than a dirty brass spittoon beside his pulpit! Today a man who can make an audience laugh and cry, who wears red socks or dresses mod might still be a sight beyond the late Sam Jones in "spirituality"—and will reach many more than will the Rev. Mr. Smith, distinguished pastor of the First Church from some adjacent town.

When meetings are scheduled with the right kind of preparation and the right kind of preachers, they still work. When they are not, they are a real embarrassment in lack of response by both friend and foe.

Having thus protected myself from the barrage of

criticism which would otherwise have resulted from this chapter, let me move on to make a very important point: *we are not innovating creative methods of reaching unbelievers in this present generation!* Ours seems to be that "in-between" age when we are running out of last century's methodology but have not yet become desperate enough in our souls to confess that we are leaving our generation practically untouched with the Gospel. As with alcoholics, so with the church: until we "bottom out" and are ready to truly admit that we have failed in our task of evangelizing this present generation, we will not become creative or God-directed, as our forefathers were.

New methods of reaching people must be a very real part of the culture of our time. We live in a skeptical, humanistic, technological society. We must begin farther back with our message to the unbeliever than was necessary in past years; we must go back as far as God Himself in our explanation of what the Christian message includes. For the first time in the history of America, we must explain why Christianity is superior to Buddhism and Hinduism to many young people who have been converted under our very noses to these Oriental faiths. They do not especially care to hear a soloist sing "The Love of God" and hear a preacher urge them to have sins forgiven; they would much prefer an opportunity to have "eyeball-to-eyeball" conversations about the entire matter, where penetrating questions can sift through the verbiage of sermons, where truth can be forced to stand simply because it is truth, not just a tear-jerking illustration.

This generation of nonchurched people is the most needy in the history of the human race! They have not found any answers, and they are looking desperately for some Way Out. In visiting a crash-pad not long ago, I was impressed by the fact that *every room* in the old, dilapidated house which was the scene of action for some fifteen or so "dropouts" from our society included at least one hand-painted picture of

Christ on the cross. Although these young people were violent in their castigations of the church, they obviously were haunted by the Christ. They are a part of the huge group of people today who are not in the slightest way interested in getting dressed up and attending a carefully designed, one-way-communication evangelistic service at a time arbitrarily set by the minister or church council.

This writer has spent countless hundreds of hours in bars, taverns, private clubs, strip-tease joints, crash pads, and in parks and picnic grounds talking to the unchurched segment of our society regarding their feelings about Christ and His Church. After years of doing this, I am absolutely convinced that the major cause for this generation's being lost to Christ is the fact that *we* are a generation of Christians without the Spirit of Christ upon us, copying an earlier generation which was led by that Spirit, copying the methods that the Spirit gave that generation, and utterly blind to the horrible tragedy we have caused by our own inept and unbroken lives.

Unless and until we "bottom out" and are ready to confess our sin of pride and self-satisfaction, all the new methods and techniques, all the gimmicks and programs, will continue to be man-made and not Spirit-given. Renewal cannot begin to commence to proceed to start in the church until the Head is given His eternal right to be the Lord of His family. Oh, Mr. Spurgeon! Did you ever imagine the jog-trot of God's people could be quite so everlasting?

14

Renewal Clues From Philosopher Hoffer

I shall forever be indebted to the man who introduced me to Eric Hoffer's writings! One cannot read his work without making endless applications of his insights to the present state of the church. In the process of reading his *True Believer,*[1] I discovered some pretty obvious things about renewal problems.

In any given structure of society, he says, there are those leaders who have struggled up from the basement of nothingness to the high tower of success. Often this has taken years and years to accomplish. They know every stone in the foundation of that structure and hold sacred every beam and board they walked on as they ascended the stairs to reach their pinnacle. They worked hard to get to "the top."

When someone comes along and suggests that the tower needs a remodeling job, he is immediately viewed as the enemy! What? Touch these sacred and hallowed walls, these foundation stones, these painfully ascended staircases? Certainly not! Does this proposer of the new not recognize the famous names of the past who helped fashion the walls? How dare he suggest renewing them?

[1]New York: Harper & Row, 1951.

Hoffer suggests that those who propose the remodeling are usually those who have not yet climbed out of the basement. They are at the beginning of their ascent to the towers. Since they have not yet invested blood, sweat, and tears in the old structure, they have no sentimental attachment to it. They evaluate it without emotion. It matters little to them whether the building stands or falls. They wish to climb up to their *own* successful position and can be pretty ruthless in doing it.

As a result, those in the basement and those in the tower become enemies of each other. The struggle begins, with upheaval and revolution. Upon a day, those in the tower are either deposed or die of natural causes, leaving the tower unoccupied. Those in the basement, previously unsentimental and unattached, move up to the tower—and become viciously defensive of the hallowed walls, foundation stones, and painfully ascended staircases! The cycle occurs again—and again.

Tensions between those in the tower and those in the basement sap much of the energy which might have been mutually invested in something truly constructive. Such tension is apparent within today's church.

I recall a minister in his early thirties who had ascended to a pinnacle of the tower in a small-sized town. He had a lovely church, a stable salary, and was reaping some of the fruits of the starvation period of his seminary years. I met him at a point in my renewal pilgrimage where a lot of good ideas, yet untried, were floating around in my mind. I shared one of them with him, seeking to evaluate its credibility to a typical minister.

The concept I reviewed with him was one we actually successfully used later in Houston. It dealt with reorganizing Bible study for adults. Instead of having traditionally divided adult classes on the basis of age and sex, I explained that a church could offer three levels of study. The individual would be allowed

125

to evaluate his own spiritual condition, and on that basis attend the class of his choice.

The first class would be an intensive year-long survey of the Scriptures for adults who did not have any background in Bible study. Upon graduating from it, the adult would be able to select from two classes, one offering depth study of an Old Testament book, the other offering study in a New Testament book. These two classes would terminate each three months, allowing members to rotate. Teachers would also rotate in teaching them, giving every instructor a time to teach, a time to be taught, and a time to really prepare for the period when he would again teach. Only gifted teachers would be invited to join the "faculty." The third class, to be taught by the pastor (the most educated Bible teacher in the church), would be an intensive topical study, requiring from each student four hours a week of study, research, and a term paper; the class would include "pop" tests and a written one-hour final exam every three months. Thus, the church would provide for all levels of spiritual development in Bible study.

When I asked the pastor what he thought of the idea, he was distressed. He responded by explaining to me that he did not feel that he could ever become involved in a program like that. It was too new, too untried, filled with too many problems. When pressed for a description of the problems, the pastor said that he had spent a long time preparing for the pastorate, and that he had a wife and children who relied on him for financial support. Some might be willing to risk their secure positions to experiment with new ideas; he did not feel he wished to do so!

Not yet thirty-five, he had already started to defend his tower. Many of those who could be most influential in the renewal of the church are precisely those who are most threatened by it. It is much less painful to doggedly preserve the status quo than to risk replacing an old beam with a new log.

It has been of interest to note that the renewal people are often formed from among those who are not yet pillars in the church, who have not yet been called to serve the First Church, who have not yet ascended to the tower.

George Bernard Shaw said, "Must a Christ die in every age for those who have no imagination?" Why, within the spiritually vital church of our Lord Jesus Christ, should the sociological principles of Hoffer prove to be so true? Should not the Body of Christ live by the principles of the Kingdom of God, rather than those of the kingdoms of this world? How can the church be viewed as a living thing without constantly changing?

The cells of the human body, we are told, are completely renewed every seven years. Bone, marrow, skin, liver, eyes, *all renewed every seven years*. Should we not be witnessing the living Christ renewing the form and shape taken by the church? Why should men of the cloth be afraid of the new, as though the word "new" were spelled "evil"? Why should any man in "high places" in God's work view himself as a "career man" and be more concerned about his reputation or his salary than about what is necessary for the church to be powerfully used by the Holy Spirit in today's world?

Hoffer's insights prove to be so true in church life! A new minister comes to church and suggests that some changes should be made. The deacons in the tower tell him of how many years the old ways have worked. He soon learns that change is not possible.

The young people return from a thrilling retreat at church camp. Many of them have started to glow with the indwelling presence of Christ. They wish to organize a prayer meeting, a street meeting, a coffee house. They face the animosity of those in the tower. They are told they are too young; they are too emotional; this will wear off in a few days. Sure enough, it does!

A layman gets an exciting idea for a new ministry. Seamen on the ships at the wharf arrive daily from across the world. Is there a way the pastor can help him organize and train a group of men to visit sailors on their ships, to distribute Scripture portions in the various languages of the world? Could they not become missionaries without ever leaving town? He faces the man in the tower. He is told that (a) there is no budget for this; (b) these men would never become a part of the local church, and we are not really reaching the people on our own church field; (c) such an idea would have to be approved by the church council; *ad infinitum*. The layman returns to his silent pew.

Renewal will not come in all its fullness to the church until those in the tower leap out to their spiritual death in Christ! When the church has leadership which has been crucified with Christ, it will have no further reputation to protect and no personal interests to shelter. Then the church will begin to move out to love the unloved.

Someone has said that there are three things true about a man on a cross: (1) he has no further personal plans; (2) he can look in only one direction; and (3) he is never going back where he came from.

When men in the church become interested in the Kingdom of God rather than their own personal kingdoms, the gates of hell are going to feel the impact!

15

An Open Letter to All Religious Weathermen and Plodders

Admittedly, this book is not being written "for all time." It is a here-and-now report on one person's view of the present state of the art in the field of church renewal. Some future reader who buys your copy of this book for a dime in some sleazy second-hand bookstore may need to be told that the Weathermen were, in our generation, a group of politically radical half-thinkers who spent their time and energy blowing up buildings and other accoutrements of our society.

Whenever I speak on renewal at a college or a seminary, I meet at least one religious Weatherman. He is a young man convinced that the new wine won't go into old skins, that the best thing that could happen to the church would be for all the stained glass walls to shatter from the explosion resulting from the organ motors shorting out. He sees the entire church of today as a complete fiasco, the greatest embarrassment that ever happened to Christ, and wishes to begin over again—from scratch.

This enlightened fellow does not have the unchristian quality of character for actually making bombs, but his words are certainly explosive. Occasionally he writes a book, suggesting how the church "ought to be." One such volume resting on my bookshelf has a magnificently absurd plan for the total restructure of the churches in a community, including the reorganization of all the clergy, the property, and the programs of all Protestant groups.

Having served just a *small* group of truly trying-hard Christians in a renewal church, I marvel at the confidence this fellow has in the human race! Those who move into renewal must realize that the place to begin is not with theory, but with people. What are people capable of being? After my forty-seven-years-in-the-ministry Dad read my original renewal document, he wrote back in all gentleness: "Son, the greatest problem I see with your experiment is *people*. They alone will determine the success of it." I smiled benignly at his remark at the time, but in the months following I have come to realize once again that he has been right about almost everything since I passed my eighteenth birthday. (It is amazing how much that man learned between my fourteenth and eighteenth years!)

It is good for all those in favor of renewing the church to look backward at *least* once a day to remember whence they came. Better yet, they should read a chapter a week in Latourette's church history. If the institutional church is all *that* bad, dear Weatherman, how is it that it brought *us* to a vital faith in the Master, and through its witness we felt God's call to serve Him? It had to be doing *something* right, or you and I would not be in the Body just now. True, it *needs* new shingles, but you cannot reroof a building whose walls have been destroyed.

Recently I was speaking in a fine congregation for an entire week regarding church renewal. The pastor had encouraged me to rattle the cages of the trapped Christians who could not see the people for the program. Along about the middle of the week, an interesting thing happened. We discovered that some of those who were in the cages were absolutely in agreement with renewal principles, but could see no more effective place for themselves in Christ's service than where they were now serving. Did we have a suggestion as to how they might more effectively serve the Lord if they abandoned their Sunday school teaching? We did not have! Many good people have already found their authentic place of ministry in Christ's name in the old, traditional patterns of church life. They do not have the imagination to live in tomorrow.

It is no *sin* to have been formed by God without a creative, imaginative bone in your body! Not everyone has the capacity to envision the new, to dream about the way it is going to be, and then set out to make the dream a reality. Along with the creative people in the world, we must also have an abundance of plodders. Without them, nothing could be accomplished. Creative people with fertile brains "climb the walls" when required to perform repetitive work; plodders are terrified by the demand to create. Those who are slow to change are not *unspiritual;* they are *plodders.*

Weathermen do not seem to understand this. If we suddenly eradicated all the buildings, programs, seminary curriculums, etc., and started all over, utterly demonic confusion would result. God-given change will always be aware of the capacities for change within human beings, as well as the crying-out needs of the human race.

Renewal must happen in stages. Those who see the need for an expanded ministry must be granted the freedom to get involved; those who are content to serve Christ with abandonment in the present structure should be allowed to do so.

Renewal will begin first in the local church among the small band of creative Christians. Not everyone has been so gifted. When we began the experimental church in Houston, I prepared a Pastor's Profile form.[1] Whenever a new member came into the fellowship, he was given a copy to fill out. After reviewing it, I spent an hour alone with each person, sharing dreams and burdens and prayers, as we learned to love each other.

One question included in the form was the result of a conference with a psychologist. I had asked this professional counselor, "How can I get a clue as to the creativity of members entering our fellowship?" After a few moments of thought, he said: "Ask them what their goals are for the next five years. Truly creative people live in the future; plodders live in the present." This question, buried in what the members eventually nicknamed my "F.B.I. Form," was extremely important to me. Again and again I authenticated the wisdom of the psychologist. The experiences of the passing months indicated that those who really *had* thought out the future were our creative people. I relied heavily on them to "dream." The remainder of the group found ministry simply in working within the *reality* of our experimental structure, but were not gifted in the area of further developing it.

A sensitive renewal leader will understand that change happens first and most easily among those who can see the future *before* it happens. For the rest, let the stained glass walls remain; let the organ play; let the Sunday school roll on!

In the church where plodders are in control, or where the minister himself is a master plodder, an explosive situation exists. Nothing is more frustrating to creative persons than to be chopped down whenever they come up with new ideas for living beyond the present! The plodders of this age have caused, single-handedly, most of the radical fringe nonchurchly renewal groups of our day to come into being. These

---

[1] Reproduced in Appendix B.

groups are often detrimental to the organized church, even though they desire to serve the same Master. They are detrimental because they tend to polarize Christians. The plodders stay within the traditional structure, and the creative persons pull away. As a result, the institutional church loses its vital, imaginative edge, tending to do over and over what it has already done well. The creative persons tend to sit on the outside and snipe at them, becoming more cynical with each nonchurch-related meeting. They come up with great ideas, but lack the platform to develop them into a "way of life" for other Christians. They need the plodders to do their "good idea" over and over patiently, to refine it and get the "bugs" out of it. Because of the schism which now exists, many of our most creative believers dissipate their concepts into thin air.

Some fellowships are fighting theological battles with each other. Some pastors have talked to me with foreboding words about how we are going to see great divisions during the seventies because of liberal and conservative theology. Perhaps so, but I feel that the next great schism that may tear apart the children of God is going to be one which crisscrosses all the levels of theology. It is going to be in the form of an even greater division between the Christians who are anxious for the church to get involved in a truly redemptive way in the changing world, and those who are thoroughly threatened by any change in the forms or structures of the church. How tragic! How awful that some believers would say, "I am of the weathermen," and others would say, "I am of the plodders." We simply *must* understand that God in divine wisdom has fitly joined all of us to each other, and that we cannot exist apart. There is no schizophrenia within the true Body. Any attempt at renewal which violates this principle of mutual love and understanding will not remain spiritually alive for long.

Do you recall the great adjustment it required to

get used to driving your new car because some of the controls were located in a different place from where they had been on the older model? I am typing this page with a new typewriter, which has the exclamation mark in a new place; it is a frustrating adjustment. Join me in cheering Robert Browning, who wrote, "I detest all change, and most a change in aught I loved long since."

When that "long since" includes the greater part of our life style, and it fades away *overnight*, how will people react? Our culture has already experienced more radical social change in the past thirty years than in the previous three hundred. Ninety percent of today's prescriptions are being filled by pharmacists with drugs not even *discovered* ten years ago! Future changes will occur at such a dizzying rate during the next thirty years that any attempts to forecast them border on the ridiculous.

Change of any sort is a threat to the security of the person. Who has not been disturbed by a new revision of the tax form, a new procedure at the office, a new rule added by the group to some simple parlor game? Inwardly, we fear we will not be adequate to succeed in untried structures, and so we shrink from them.

The agony of change is rooted deep within the human personality. We tend to live in the world of activities we enjoy and the more we have already practiced something, the more we enjoy it. We are the creation of our yesterdays. We enjoy certain foods because we have eaten them from childhood. We enjoy certain forms of worship because we have shared them from childhood. They are comfortable.

In the yesterdays of life we accomplished certain tasks and failed in the achievement of others. As a result, we learned self-assurance from the achieved tasks and fear of the new from the failures. We developed a sense of personal identity: "I swim better than most people, but sing worse than most." The longer we live, the more we discover about ourselves, and we live more and more in the area of successfully achieved activities. With age, we find it more and more threatening to explore the spaces of the un-achieved, choosing rather to redo the things we have already done well.

For those who enter adulthood without significant areas of childhood achievement, *any* change poses a great threat. Such people will withdraw when any change is proposed, and may be viciously critical, hoping to buttress their own self-identity by pointing out the flaws in the plans for the new, the innovative.

A friend of mine is in the business of purchasing small banks. He buys the ones with large cash balances, which he uses to purchase still more banks. One day at lunch he said to me, "When I am offered a bank, I ask only one question: 'How old is the president?' You see, I have discovered that if the age of the president is in the forties or early fifties, the bank will have 90% or more of its cash loaned out. But if the president is in his sixties, invariably the bank will have from 45 to 55% of its available cash un-invested. I buy banks run by old men." The older we get, the less we desire to innovate. We increasingly desire only the secure pattern, the tried method, the traditional structure.

Lives there a minister with experience so limited that he has not discovered the wrath which descends from tampering with an old, sacred order of service? It is agonizingly hard for the church to change! Even for the most dedicated, the human factor of insecurity in an untried structure must be overcome by great discipline.

A church should not change just to be different. It should change because the context of culture about it requires it to restructure so the people of God can be redemptive in their life and witness. Change merely for the sake of change is destructive! If the logic and clear purpose of change are not comprehended by those required to participate, the backlash can be disastrous.

But, having laid forth that caution, it must be clearly stated that the church *must change!* Half of today's world population has been born since the end of World War II. It took a million years for the world population to reach the one billion mark in A.D. 1780. In the next 167 years, the world's population more than tripled. *And now it will take only 15 years to add the next billion!* This new, young world of humanity has a different set of values, a different type of music, a different form of narcotic to escape from the pressures of reality. They will not be reached easily by last century's methods. For those who have experienced every level of emotion during the childhood watching of T.V. newscasts and movies, Pollyanna illustrations and death-bed scenes in the minister's sermons are more amusing than convicting. Today's modern is not nearly as absorbed with what will happen in the hereafter as was the generation just deceased. Far more worrisome is the terror of living on a planet with immediate ecological problems, an immediate death to be faced in a war not clearly understood, and the anxieties caused by a dehumanizing, depersonalized society.

The church that continues to talk about the problems that haunted yesterday's generation will find little audience in today's world. Nor will it *have* an audience, as it did yesterday, if it insists that people must attend the Sunday service at the sanctuary. Ours is a mobile world. Weekends are filled with pleasure-bound apartment dwellers headed for the beach, the mountains or the old home town. They are no longer available for church services as they have been in past years. Professional football games attract many who find attending this new Sunday activity far more satisfying than the older Sabbath social structure of Sunday school and worship service. (The cost of the football game is also considerably less than a tithe of one's income!)

The church of today *must change*—but that change must be clearly directed by the Spirit of God, and it must take into account the problems of adjustment required by those who have found a measure of security, not only in their God, but also in their church as a social structure of life.

16

The Church As Linus' Blanket

We are all indebted to the Peanuts comic strip for making us see ourselves as we really are. Sometimes I think some churches are best described by the child-blanket carried about by Linus. No matter how strange the changing world, his little blanket is a reminder of his past—the crib and the bottle—and somehow, he cannot give it up. He takes his little patch of security wherever he goes.

For some years I served my denomination in a section of the nation which was new to its work. During those years, I observed a heartbreaking phenomenon. Many displaced persons, relocated in a new section of the nation, mourned for the old familiar forms of culture they had known "back home." It was not just that the climate was radically changed or that the people spoke with strange accents. The foodstuffs on the shelves in the grocery stores did not include the common items eaten "back home." Strange names appeared in the telephone book, denoting ancestries from European nations which had not settled in their old home towns. Even gasoline stations had new names. All the old, comfortable forms of community life were gone. These dear people, so alone and so unhappy, needed a security, a Linus' blanket, to which they might cling.

How could they sing the Lord's songs in a strange land? Even churches of their own theological spectrum were "different." They did not use the old organizations, the old patterns for worship. Change, to be sure, was a miserable commodity in their lives, because there was so much of it.

As a result, they organized a church. It was just *exactly* like the one back home, complete with hymnals, attendance boards on either side of the choir loft, and usually an imported minister with the "right" accent.

Certainly not all, but some, of these churches revealed a genuine disinterest among the members toward the evangelism of residents who had been born and raised in the area. Often there was an absence of a compassionate zeal to share Christ with those who lived in an otherwise unchurched community. Some pastors would tell me of driving after out-of-state automobiles with the "right" license tags from "back home," certain that at last they had found a newcomer in the community who would want to join their church.

This picture is not true of all the churches which formed during the early "pioneer missions" days of my ministry. Some of the most dedicated, godly lay men and women I shall ever know began to serve the Lord with authentic love in their hearts in those areas. But some of those churches came into being through people who wanted a bit of the old culture in the strange land. For them, the church was not as much an organism of Christ's Body as it was a sociological structure, a social form from "down home."

How far can the church go in allowing this sort of thing? How much of an obligation do churches have to those who need the security of the old forms, the old structures? Those "down home" churches are, in fact, an attestation of the fact that change is a terrible, threatening thing to accept, and they suggest that many of our unchanging church forms have precious little to do with the theology of a group of people or with a redemptive mission. Many church-goers place their trust not so much in God, but in the forms that have communicated God from childhood.

Examine the churches about you. Within many cities will be found congregations who have copied their rural counterparts and thus attract their members because country folk who come to live in the city feel "at home" there. I recall pondering many weeks over the reasons behind the successful growth of a certain large church in a city which was rapidly becoming a sophisticated, depersonalized community. It became obvious that the church growth was simply the result of the church staff capitalizing on being "country" in the city. Located in the heart of the Bible belt, it was performing exactly the same cultural function as the churches I had seen in other distant areas of the nation!

Seldom does a congregation like this experience renewal. Such churches are predicated on the preservation of the past, genuinely hostile to the innovative. They are a Linus' blanket, a little haven of the past in the midst of a new day, a new culture.

One wonders if, in our age, the loyalty of many church members to their denomination may be understood more on the basis of fear of the new than upon theological commitment. Most of the laymen I have talked to within my denomination have precious little knowledge of their church's theology, let alone a commitment to it. Why, then, do they always seek out a church of their own denomination when moving to a new town? If it is not made on the basis of biblical truth and theological dimension, what is left but loyalty to forms of church structure? It is simply a bit of security in a new community to step into a congregation where they worship just like "back home."

If I ever had any doubts about this premise, my ministry in Houston shattered them forever! Our congregation was unequivocally committed to the statement of faith adopted by sister churches. We fully cooperated with the support of missionary causes sponsored by the denomination, and I was well known for my love for and activity in the national body.

When members of our denomination, having newly moved into our community, would come to visit us in our services, we would offer to visit in their homes and explain the experimental nature of our life. We would explain that we had carefully preserved the *purposes* of the traditional organizations, but had restructured them to become an experimental church.

Following that discussion, eight out of ten of these people would join a wonderfully alive and committed sister church in our area which carried on its work, using the old, familiar forms of church structure. Again and again I left the homes of these new families, fully aware that the sole reason they rejected becoming a part of us was that we threatened them terribly by being "different." They could not face the terrifying readjustment to the new structure! We might as well have been theologically Buddhist; *they needed the old forms to find God.*

As the American culture explodes with rapid change, more and more people will cling to the church, wanting it to be a bit of "yesterday" in "tomorrow." The church has the unique distinction of being just about the only social form left in America which can be manipulated by its members to remain where they want it to remain. Will churches and pastors be able to reject the strong temptation to acquiesce to the degrading role of a Linus' blanket? In an age of increasing doubt and secularism, this could be one of the simplest escape mechanisms available—but "old shoe" churches seldom attract unbelievers.

If the church prostitutes its role as a living, breathing redemptive Body to offer a bit of yesterday to the people who fear change, it will find God's finger writing "Ichabod" over its door!

141

Speaking from that collegiate cynicism reserved, it seems, for sophomores, one university student said bitterly, "The church I come from was *dragged,* kicking and screaming, into the twentieth century!" As he expounded with illustrations, I tuned in to his attitude instead of his words. His was clearly a statement of hurt disappointment rather than anger or resentment. In truth, he dearly loved the congregation he was castigating.

His pain came from the discovery that his local church was not a vital part of the world about it, but was a Linus' blanket group. It had not done a thing to prepare him to live in a humanistic university. He was frustrated that his minister did not really seem to care as much about *people* as about the budget and the enlargement of the membership. He was disillusioned that so many unbelievers on his campus were ready to become radically, fanatically committed to political causes, while the local denominational group of collegians often seemed content to recline through vesper services held at hours convenient for the "truly devout." He was irritated at the decision of the members of his home church to beautify their church grounds at a cost approximating the full annual salaries of sixty missionaries. His pain was caused by the fact that, in an age of suffering and confusion, his home church turned into a monastic, self-centered congregation of people who met to withdraw from the nasty and the dirty, and who were not reflecting the true nature of the Body of Christ.

Churches must stiffly resist this temptation to serve as havens from the secular world. Nevertheless, they have an obligation to minister to all those within the fellowship, and this includes the fearful, the weak, the carnal, *and the insecure who need a Linus' blanket.*

It seems to me that this fact has been overlooked by most of the authors who wrote the books on renewal which occupy my shelves. The church cannot renege on its obligation to be the redemptive force to the half-redeemed. Soren Kirkegaard was right when he suggested that fifty sincere Christians were not equaled by one hundred "twaddlers"; but any genuine, God-given pattern of renewal has got to show compassion for the twaddlers in the church as well as for the sinners outside the walls. This may well be the most serious problem facing the renewing church in this age: changing its forms to be really witnessing to its society, it must at the same time accept its obligation to redeem all the twaddlers.

17

See All the People

Remember the little hand game we played as kids?
Fingers bent inside the palms, hidden; thumbs held
together to be the church doors; index fingers form
a church steeple; hands then turned inside out, with
fingers revealed; done to the recitation of the poem

> Here's the church,
> Here's the steeple.
> Open the doors,
> See all the people!

Ugh!

With such horrible theology converted into a child's
game, is it any wonder we have such a problem with
genuine biblical fellowship in today's church? Is it
really hard to understand why we have so many un-
moving twaddlers in every existing congregation?

As a seminary student pastor, I can recall the
disillusionment that used to sweep over me during
the offertory as I waited for the time to stand and
preach. I would look over a group of people who
were typical of many churches in our day. Ten percent gave ninety percent of the money; fifteen percent held all the offices of the church; only two percent
had ever even *tried* to lead a friend to Christ. Sixty
percent of the members would not do one more religious thing, in public or private, in worship or in

prayer, until next Sunday morning's worship service. Thirty percent of those members bothered to *attend* only when it suited them to do so. I would look into those faces and ask myself in amazement, "Why in the world do we remain together? We have nothing in common, save the cultural obligation to attend service on Sunday morning."

Some of the men had frankly told their men's class teacher that the only reason they attended his class was out of personal obligation to their wives. We did not really care about each other; we did not love or understand each other; we did not share a common commitment to the Lordship of Christ within our lives. *Why were we there?*

I learned how to write *koinonia* in Koine during those same months in the seminary, but the expression of it within my congregation was still untranslatable Greek to me when I got my degree!

Consider the polarization of people in the church today. You have the *Good Guys Who Wear White Hats.* They are all hard at their tasks within the program, doing all the work in matters of teaching, stewardship, policy making, praying, and everything else required to keep the church running. The pastor spends most of his time with them, since he is the *Head Knocker of the Program* and must direct them. The good guys get to know each other pretty well through all this involvement, and as a result they go on picnics together, play parlor games, and "drop in" on each other after church services are completed.

Then you have the *Dirty Hypocrites Who Go to the Bar on Saturday and Church on Sunday.* My, how they are despised! They are considered a disgrace to God and, even worse, to "our population." Fact of the matter is, they don't really attend church on Sunday much at all. They have their names on the roll, but that's about all you can say for them.

Consider the manner by which the polarization reveals itself. Here's a chunk of conversation synthesized from many life situations.

> SCENE: *a deacon's meeting, during the coffee break following a lengthy discussion about paving the parking lot.*

DEACON B: Did you see in the paper that the Bill Problems got a divorce? You know, they are still carried on our church roll. Boy! That's a poor testimony for our church in the community, isn't it?

DEACON C: I'll tell you something even worse. You know old George Wino who got saved and baptized during that revival we had two years ago and came to our men's fish fry with alcohol on his breath right after that? Well, he was listed in the paper among people arrested this past week for drunken driving. Something should be done about members like him. I always have felt the evangelist used too much emotion in his preaching that year. He got so many people drifting in that my family actually had to stand up one night while he preached. These people don't "stick" from meetings like that.

DEACON D: Are you *sure* the Problems you mentioned are members of our church? I don't recall ever meeting them in my job as greeter on Sunday morning.

DEACON A: No, you wouldn't meet them then. Like so many members we have on our roll, they haven't been around the church for months. But let me tell you something. The Bill Problems live across the street from us, and we have known for a long time they were not getting along. They really scream at each other, and in the summertime when the windows are open they are heard by all the neighbors. I told my wife to stay away from that mess over there. You know, somebody should try to help those people before one of them kills the other! Guess divorce is better than a murder.

CHAIRMAN: Well, fellows, if you are finished with your coffee break, let's get back to the salt mine. We still have to discuss janitorial supplies, and we have a request from the ladies to increase our foreign missions gift this year by twenty-five percent. Got a lot of business ahead, and we need to get home at a decent time from this meeting.

DEACON C: Right! Let's get back to the Lord's work.

In between these two poles of good guys and bad guys (you figure out for yourself which is which!) are Soren Kierkegaard's twaddlers. They are the bland, half-committed ones who are better known for their shades of pure gray than either black or white. They represent the great majority. Some of them are teachers in the primary department, and get to know a few other members in passing as the result of attending teachers' meetings—but not too intimately, mind you!

"Open the doors, and see all the people!" Any resemblance between *this* and the Church of our Lord Jesus Christ is absolutely ridiculous.

Dr. Robert G. Lee once preached to a group of ministers a sermon entitled, "If the gold rusts, what will the iron do?" When a situation like the one just described exists, much of the problem frequently lies with clergymen who are in the midst of their stone-stepping "careers" from the country pastorates to the large and influential pulpits. The stones they step on are not made of granite, but human bones.

One such dear brother told me in the middle stage of his "career" some years ago that he had done considerable research and had concluded that the amount of time a minister spends in visiting his people has no influence whatsoever on the church's rate of growth. He quoted another well-known Winner who had told him in private he never visited any members unless they were sick or dying, and that his congregation had been told before he was called that he was, in fact, a "pulpit" preacher and not a "visiting" preacher. This authenticated my friend's research: his role as a minister would be a pulpit one, with long hours spent in the study. He did not feel an intimate relationship with his people would add anything, and after all, familiarity *does* breed contempt!

Actually, there is something that would have been added to his members. *That addition would have been the very real Spirit of Christ, without which the Church cannot live and breathe!*

147

If the church is connected to Christ, it will be marked first of all by *koinonia*—fellowship. *Koinonia* is a relationship of love and intimate intertwining of believers, a spiritual connection of real people who are in fellowship with Christ because they have seen Him at work in the lives of the rest of the group. Take this away, and the church does not exist. It is not then an organism, but an organization. It may have walls and programs, but it will not be experiencing that oneness that exists when Christ flows through other members of the Body into us, and vice versa. When He releases us from the bondage of alienation from the Father, we are released to be genuinely attached to others who are our brothers and sisters in Him. This attachment occurs as the gift of the Cross.

Handshaking and sipping soft drinks does not approximate this relationship of *koinonia*. It takes place as we are willing to be real people to each other.

Someone has suggested that most of us have three persons in our bodies. First, there is the ugly, black monster that lives within us. It thinks ugly thoughts, says nasty things, lusts, hates, and acts in such a disgusting way that we are very much ashamed of it. As a result, the second person develops in our lives: the false face—a mask of sweetness and light that we wear to varying degrees before those who are not intimate enough with us to get acquainted with the monster. Those within our house see right through the false face image we put on, but they will not "tell on us," because *we* know all about *their* false faces and monsters, too.

The third image is the real me, who is the result of the chaining of the monster by the power of the indwelling Christ. Given the forgiveness of God from the *penalty* of sin, His indwelling Presence also brings us to the *power* over the monster for the first time in our lives. There is no real need to keep flashing the false face, since the real me has come to exist in us. Nevertheless, the habit of using it is strong. It is so much easier to keep playing the little part with others than to face the stress of *change*. Besides, there is the haunting fear that if people got to know the real me, they might not be as impressed by it as by the false face.

If we only realized how phony the false face appears to others in the first place, we would not be so hesitant to abandon it! It appears most false when we don it to impress others with our spirituality or when we wear it to "testify" about how *great* it is to be a Christian.

What happens when the Reverend wears his false face all the time, and the members wear their false faces to church, to Sunday school, and to choir practice? Why, you have the False Face Church; *open the doors, and see all the people!*

One of the contradictions of life to me has been this fear of the redeemed to be "real me's" with each other. Mind you, although I have spent more than a minister's share of time in bars, it has been *as a minister,* not as a dirty hypocrite. (I just happen to believe that when the One who was a friend of wine-bibbers and sinners comes to abide within, to be so *insulated* makes it unnecessary to be *isolated.*) In those bars I have discovered an interesting thing about sinners. They have an amazing penchant for being honest about what they are. I have had married men tell me about the girl they visit in an apartment. One described to me his very illegal plan of cheating on his income tax. A prostitute made no bones about the reality of her profession. Glimmers of the honesty to be found in a bar are astounding!

I have also been deeply impressed by what goes on in an Alcoholics Anonymous meeting. You enter a very smoky room, where everyone is on the same level of relationship—first-name. You sit down in a folding chair, and some fellow stands up and gives out a "chip" to a woman who has stayed sober for a whole month. The "chip" has written on one side:

149

"ONE DAY AT A TIME." Someone else named Phil blows out the one candle on a birthday cake, and everyone eats a bite to celebrate one full year of sobriety in his struggle with liquor. Then Harold stands up. Bless his heart, he plumb forgot to wear his false face, and he starts right out with the astonishing statement before all the listeners, "My name is Harold, and I am an alcoholic." He goes on to tell about all those miserable years he spent as a slave to "white lightning," of his homes (plural) that were lost to buy booze, of a faithful wife who put up with all those monkeyshines, and finally he says a good word for Roger, sitting over in the corner, who got up at 3 a.m. and came over to walk the floor a few nights ago when Harold was about to "cave in" and take a snort. One is amazed by the honesty to be found among these ex- and not-so-ex-drunks.

One sits down in the counseling room of a Crusade and listens quietly to the conversations going on between seekers and helpers. "The first step in becoming a Christian," says the helper, "is to admit you are a sinner. Until you are ready to confess that, there is nothing God can do for you. Are you willing just now to admit to God that you have sinned?" *That* requires an honest answer, now doesn't it?

I recall a recent service in which I spoke as a guest minister. The song leader was one of those naive fellows who had not yet been "burned" by the embarrassment of what was about to happen to him. He stopped the previous hymn with a wide wave of his hand, and with a Pepsodent flash said, "Who has a testimony to give for the Lord? Who'll be first?" One could feel the temperature rise from body heat as the silence deepened. The false faces had been unfairly summoned, just as everyone had settled back into limbo for a special number and the sermon! It took a few moments for the group to decide how to handle this unexpected threat. Some settled the matter by deciding to keep quiet, no matter how long it took to make their point. Finally, one dear brother unfolded from the seat, false face hastily adjusted, and said, "Jesus is all the world to me. I never miss a chance to say a word for my Lord. He has been mighty good to my family and me, and I just want all of you to know who are here tonight unsaved and hellbound, that you would sure be better off if you took that first step towards God and joined the church like I did." With a few benign smiles from those who had been let off the hook by his pat response, the song leader wiped away the nervous perspiration, and the special number came up.

The games Christians play!

Renewal in the church requires men and women to be redeemed—*and only as redeemed as they really are!* It is only at the level of gut-honesty that we can see God working in our midst. When this is forfeited in favor of impressing others with how "spiritual" we are when at the church house, we destroy the very Body of Christ. How much different that meeting could have been if the dear brother would have stood up to say, "My name is Bill, and I am a sinner. I run a local gasoline station in this town, and, well, you fellows know how men like to swap dirty jokes when they are away from women. This has been a real problem for me since becoming a Christian. It's hard to change the habits of half a lifetime, but the Lord living inside me keeps doing these fantastic things in my life down there at the station. Like just yesterday. I found myself listening to one of my men cutting loose with a real corker. A chunk of the old lust in me said, 'You can just sit here and work on the books, and act like you can't hear what's going on, and take it in anyhow. No one will notice.' Then, I heard the Master say, 'Bill, get me out of here!' Well, I just got up and walked out to the wash rack until I heard the gravel in their laugh. I guess there is always gravel in the laugh when there is dirt in the joke. Then I went back in and sat down at the desk again. My man looked at me kind of funny, but we were busy and he had to catch a car. Well, a little later he came to me and apologized for the joke. I told him it wasn't the joke that bothered me. It was Christ who had made me get up and leave. I wanted him to know that I loved him a whole lot and that I wasn't mad at him for what he had said. My problem was that since the Lord had come to live inside me, I just have to be obedient to Him. Actually, I had to admit I wanted to hear the end of the story as *Bill,* but as one who had been invaded by Christ, I had no control over the situation. Folks, I sure would appreciate it if you would continue to pray for this old sinner. It doesn't always work out like that in my life, but I sure am willing for it to happen more often."

How much more alive things are when the real me stands up! That's the way the Lord of the Church wants things to happen. Feelings are not always on the positive side within the believer, and we are utterly false when we simulate a life in which nothing is *ever* wrong. Children see the inner ugliness of moms and dads in the home, and watch them wear their piety at church; it makes fine atheists out of them when they become adults.

It would be impossible to count the number of church splits and fights I have observed during the past years. Again and again, the False Face Church faces a situation in which, in spite of everything, the monsters come out of their dens and roar like old Beelzebub himself. The whole community then realizes how phony the whole situation has been; a generation is seldom long enough for the Lord's work to recover from the damage done.

Good old Charlie Brown has said so significantly: "I love humanity; it's people I can't stand." Many a church member could paraphrase this: "I love my church; it's the membership I can't stand." But that whole concept is in error theologically, for the church is *people,* even as their love for each other is *fellowship.* When we exist apart from each other even while sharing the same classes, pews, and choir selections, we are not the true church at all!

To become a body of loving, interrelated men and women is the first and foremost task of believers. To share each other's burdens means that we must be willing to unburden the problems to be shared. To pray for one another means we must share our prayer needs. People who simply laugh together and who do not know how to weep together never learn how to love together. Those who maneuver themselves into some "high office" in the church as an ego-feeding status symbol will never be able to be gut-honest with others about themselves. Those who hate their brother must understand that John says quite clearly they have no claim to represent themselves as the children of God. We must understand that the church is not a *sanctuary* full of people. It is a family of God, in which each one risks being exactly what he is—half redeemed, half sinning, half-full of faith, half-full of doubts. The Christian who has not yet learned how to say to a fellow traveler: "The Christ who lives in me greets the Christ who lives in you," has some blessed days ahead! I so gratefully introduce the members of West Memorial to guest ministers with the statement: "I want you to meet the people to whom I minister—and who minister to me."

I recall a particular Wednesday evening when our little trio of pastor, pastor's wife, and mother-in-law were late for prayer meeting at the Capps' house. I kept calling to the two women to get ready and come out to the car, since we were very late. There followed some motor gunning, some horn blowing, and two very distressed women got into the car. As we screeched away from the curb with some well-placed comments from the Reverend about how disgusting it was to have to walk in late, the minister's spouse had some pretty pointed retorts. Mother-in-law finally suggested halfway to prayer meeting that we let her out so that she could walk back home. This request was summarily denied, and we arrived some five minutes late for the service of prayer. Wearing our false faces, the three members joyfully greeted the group as though heaven had just come down and glory had filled our souls. What else would you expect from the Very Reverend and his immediate family?

The hypocrisy of it all flooded over me, until I just could not stand it any longer. As we sat down and the group got quiet, awaiting the first pearls of truth in the Bible study, I explained to them what had happened on the way to the meeting, turned to my sweet wife, asked her to forgive me for being such a bear, and we made up right in front of the whole group.

I was, and am, grateful for the relationship with a group of people who do not expect false piety where true piety does not exist, and who are such sinners themselves that they can understand sin in the lives of others. One couple in the group that night later came privately to tell me that our display of honesty about the little spat had given them renewed relationships of communication in their own marriage. The example of a couple making up after a tiff had been a witness to them that their own marriage did not have to remain stalemated because of pride and refusal to admit wrong.

The unexpected result of the honest exchange of words in front of the group made me realize again that we often discover just how alive Christ is by seeing Him work in the biggest messes of life. Simple openness with each other allows these revelations of Christ's work to travel laterally between members of the family of God.

We are not just "people"; we are very real, truly problemed persons, who are in the process of *being saved* by the living, powerful Christ. Those who are not experiencing this in their fellowship are being robbed of the pearl of great price.

Ministers who live in their pious little ivory towers, who refuse to weep with the hurt, agonize with the lonely, and listen to the problems of their flock, who spend their time in the books and the pulpit, are specifically a part of what is most wrong with the church of today. That sort of ministry, if it ever was needed, is in sore need of a first-class burial in today's society! One West Coast newspaper had advertised in its personal column a "Listening Service." For a charge of twenty-five dollars per hour, the ad explained, an untrained person will come to your home and just *listen* to your problems. Carefully advertised, these people made no pretense about having any professional training in counseling, nor wisdom for providing adequate solutions to the problems. *They just listen!* How can a man be an authentic representative of the Lord in a day and age like this who is "too busy" to listen to bleeding hearts? What Scriptural basis is there for a man who can claim from the pulpit the greatest love in all the world and who is not willing on a personal basis to be available to love?

To understand these matters is to get a real clue about the answer to the situation existing between the church members who wear black, gray, or white hats. We have no right to polarize, to form little cliques of "do-gooders" and "do-badders" and "do-nothingers." A vital, open, honest interrelationship is required between those in the Body.

This truth really exploded into life for me some years ago while preaching at a revival meeting in a middle-sized church. The minister shared with me his dilemma concerning the "dead wood" in the membership. He had written these people, some of whom had been delinquent members for years, begging them to come back. Telephone calls had been made. Deacon visitations had proved fruitless. What could be done?

Securing the names of eight such representative

families, I asked permission to interview them as an "outsider" to discover if there was something which might be done. In the first home, I noted a mantle full of bowling trophies. These people were avid bowlers and spent most of their spare time bowling. They were active, all right, but not in the church. The next home had a problem in it, which easily surfaced in the conversation. Dad had lost his job, and the family had gone seven months without income. They could not contribute to the church because of this, and so they simply dropped out. Feeling that if you can't pay your way you should not expect "services," the church had been dropped.

In every one of those visits, I found the same thing to be true: not one of those families had a single close friendship developed within the church! Without exception, every family had a complete set of friends, activities, and relationships outside the membership of that church.

I also discovered the keys to reaching them, so obvious and evident from the cursory visits made in their homes. The key to the first family was bowling; to the second, it was assistance in finding a job; in other homes, it was an interest in fishing, auto racing, sewing, teen-age problems.

The suggestion was made to the minister that all eight of the families could undoubtedly be brought back into fellowship in the church if some specific families would be willing to develop friendships with them. Alas! The honest attempt of the minister to find eight families in the white hat group who would take time to love some delinquent members proved to be fruitless. They did not have the desire, time, or concern to invest the necessary hours to love, share, fish, bowl, sew, and become friends with these people.

This polarization of church members and their refusal to be open, honest, and truly concerned about each other is one of the most serious difficulties facing the restoration of members presently uninvolved in churches. It stems from the church not being the Body of Christ.

In contrast, I recall a fine young woman in Houston who was swimming through some pretty murky waters and came to me for counseling. Because she had shared her problem with me, I agonized over her need in prayer, and at her request shared a part of the need with a handful of others who joined me in intercession for her. One Sunday evening our fellowship had just convened when she slipped in and took a seat. The fellowship time included conversational prayer, but she did not say a word. Before we broke up, she quietly slipped out without a comment to anyone.

The following week in our counseling session, I remarked about how pleased I had been to see her slip in to our fellowship, but that I regretted not being able to greet her afterwards. She replied, "Well, I was going through a deep depression that evening and felt that I would be overwhelmed. I didn't hear a single word of your message, and I could not bring myself to say a word to anyone. I just needed to be with someone who cared a whole lot that night, so I came. I was ministered to by those who sat silently around me; I knew that they really did love me and were earnestly praying for me. That was all I needed. I left feeling as refreshed as though I had slept all night, and the depression was gone!"

How beautiful! The People Who Care had ministered just by *being the Body* for the ever-present, indwelling Christ. Their very presence had reached out and nonverbally brought healing to one in our midst. The church was authentic that night; it was used in the Christ-way that night.

Why should we settle for any less than this? Why should we live in the substrata of relationships, when it is so much more exciting and blessed to live on the level of the real person?

18

What Do We Do About the Twaddlers?

When I first began to dream of pastoring an experimental church, I had been greatly influenced by the renewal authors. Their books filled about eight feet of shelf, and I had avidly read them all. One note seemed to be sounded over and over: we must make membership in a church *mean something;* people would amount to much more for God if their church membership required more of them. I found myself swept along by this philosophy and visited several churches where they had, in fact, toughened church membership. Although I observed some who leaned toward the heresy of the Pharisees among those who thanked God they were not like others, I was still impressed by the fact that a Christian had a much harder time joining the Kiwanis Club than the average church and accepted a much greater discipline when becoming a Rotarian than he ever did when becoming a Baptist! Surely Christ demanded more of those who were to take up their cross and follow Him than what the traditional church membership standards expected.

Clearly, I thought, the renewed church had to get tough about who joined the Body! I scrutinized those groups who required up to two years of training before taking the final vows. The first sixty-four-page manuscript I wrote on the subject suggested that every member of the experimental church should be required to (1) tithe, (2) complete a full six-month training program before becoming eligible for membership, and (3) assume a task of ministry at the time their full membership was granted.

I had completely eliminated the twaddlers!

Room was provided for the thoroughly committed believer, space was offered to the atheist and alcoholic in our structure, and a place was available for the baby Christian who desired to grow rapidly into the fullness of Christ. No place at all had been provided for those long-term Christians who were barely committed to Christ—and they represent about 70% of the total Christian community! The reaction to my paper by those professional Christians (preachers!) who reviewed my document was unanimously favorable: they felt this single stroke of membership policy would solve all the ills of the church. What we needed to do was to get tough with the twaddlers: they could get in or out, but they would not be allowed to continue to twaddle!

The only problem which developed in the actual practice of my theory was that no one had alerted the twaddlers to the new principle. They were quite content to go on with their part-time commitment to Christ, and it bothered them no more to *not* be able to join the church than it was bothering them that they were church members not serving Christ. They just joined some other traditional congregation, and that was that.

In my visitation to the initial members of the West Memorial group who called me to be their pastor, I met Gene and Mary. They were quite frank in confessing to me that they were not to be considered totally committed Christians. With their marvelous penchant for shocking honesty, they began to enumerate their "sins," no doubt expecting me to be shocked. I do not know what they thought I was thinking, but

159

they could not have started to read my mind! Were not these two marvelous persons who had so many rough edges in their spiritual lives truly genuine twaddlers? What a shock. I began to realize that I had already fallen deeply in love with them, and I could see so many potentially exciting things God was going to do with them in the days ahead. Well, perhaps *just this once* we could overlook the great renewal principle for the sake of their need; I would put them in the category of the pagan, which would allow me to identify with them. In the future, no more twaddlers; they had come in by accident, so we would make the best of it.

But they were most certainly *not* pagans! They were twaddlers—good, God-fearing, half-committed, casual, undependable, preoccupied, long-term Christians. God used them to teach me some principles of renewal that were not in the books.

I discovered that they were quite, quite available for a remodeling job by the Holy Spirit. What they needed most was not a discipline to "shape up," but some bushel baskets full of love and care. We shared many a cup of coffee together, cried some, laughed lots. Others in the church, truly committed, fell just as much in love with them as I had, and Gene and Mary began to explode into Christian commitment. The secret of reaching the twaddlers had not one thing to do with membership; it had to do with *love,* with *fellowship.*

Gene and Mary took on new names and faces in the months ahead as new twaddlers came to us. Many of them were initially looking for a Linus' blanket church, unwilling to become involved as witnessing Christians in their world. We let them know that membership in our group demanded commitment, but gradually we learned to define what we meant by "commitment." We explained that it meant that we were, each of us, at some stage of our spiritual pil-

160

grimage, and "commitment" meant simply to be unwilling to sit down and rest at this stage.

Suddenly the twaddlers disappeared! They were not really a bunch of disgustingly half-committed believers at all; they were our brothers and sisters in the family of God, walking over the ground of the pilgrimage that some others of us had already trod. They were available to the Lord *where they were* and could begin to serve Him *where they were*.

I began to preach this new renewal principle from the pulpit. We did not have to wait until we reached some "level" of commitment before beginning to share our faith. *Any* believer, regardless of how undeveloped or uncommitted, had Christ lodged in his heart—and that meant he had ten million percent more in his life than the most pious pagan he met! Why not encourage him to share what he could of Christ from wherever he was in his pilgrimage?

Daniel T. Niles has suggested that a proper definition for evangelism is "one hungry beggar telling another hungry beggar where to find bread." We are *all* hungry beggars, and any beggar with the bread is ahead of one without a morsel. God began to make me see that we did not have to make a person a master baker before he was qualified to distribute the bread.

This revolutionary truth allowed us to live under grace, not law. We still offered the six-month training course "expected" of each sincere member, but we also realized that taking the course was not a cure-all. The remedy was love and involvement with the twaddler. As he watched others around him burning with Christ's flame, he soon decided that he wanted to burn brighter himself. We had no place for the yesterday or for the Linus' blanket concept in our fellowship. The twaddler never realized this; he was too busy soaking up the individual love and attention he was getting from the group. His spiritual change was not painful, for he was surrounded by people who *had* changed, and they were so attractive with

161

the loveliness of Christ in them that spiritual growth
naturally occurred.

West Memorial adopted a Covenant which is actually a rewrite of a statement written by members
of the Church of the Savior in Washington, D.C.:

> In the spirit of love, we have banded together to
> comprise a local expression of an ecclesia, which is
> the body of those on whom the call of God rests
> to witness to the grace and truth of God.
>
> Because we believe that Jesus is the Christ, the
> Son of the living God, we will seek to bring every
> phase of our lives under His Lordship.
>
> We unreservedly and with abandon commit our
> lives and destiny to Christ, promising to give Him
> priority in all the affairs of life. We will seek first
> the Kingdom of God and His righteousness.
>
> We believe that God is the total owner of our
> lives and resources. We give God the throne in
> relation to the material aspects of our lives. Because
> God is a lavish giver, we too shall be lavish and
> cheerful in our regular gifts.
>
> We commit ourselves, regardless of the expendi-
> tures of time, energy, and money to become in-
> formed, mature Christians.
>
> We will seek to be Christ-led in all relations with
> our fellowmen, with other nations, groups, classes,
> and races.
>
> We commit ourselves to watch over one another
> in brotherly love; to pray for each other; to aid
> one another in sickness and distress.
>
> We recognize that the function of this ecclesia
> is to glorify God in adoration and sacrificial service,
> and to be God's missionaries in the world, bearing
> witness to God's redeeming grace in Jesus Christ.

On the anniversary of the church, each member is
given opportunity to renew his membership covenant
vow. It is so written that the twaddlers understand
there is plenty of room for them in the fellowship of
believers.

At this point, I have decided that a true definition
for a twaddler is "anyone who has not traveled along
the pilgrimage quite as far as I." This being the case,
I, too, am a twaddler, for many have walked far

past me. To them, *I* must be a real embarrassment to the Kingdom!

I wonder if Soren Kierkegaard ever realized what a big old twaddler he would have looked like to Paul.

19

Church Buildings: Tools or Toys?

A large portion of money given by God's people these days is being spent for church buildings. Should you examine the budgets of typical urban churches, you will most likely discover that 50% or more of the weekly incomes are being spent for this purpose. Don't stop with the mortgage payment; add to it the cost for janitorial and maintenance salaries, insurance, heat, light, etc. The conclusion one comes to is that the Kingdom of God is being established as real estate!

Churches in the United States now own in excess of $102 billion in land and buildings. I am not picking on my denomination, but simply using it as an example: we will spend far more than $50 million this year *simply to pay the interest on church mortgages.* This profit by bankers from churches represents an investment which is several million dollars more than the amount to be invested by those churches for all home and foreign mission causes. We are not only spending more money on ourselves than on evangelizing the heathen, but we are giving more of it to pay the salaries of our bankers than all of the salaries of our world missionary force!

All this would be disturbing even if we were growing in impact because of our brick and mortar holdings. A recent poll indicates religion in America is losing ground *five times faster now than in 1957.* Our buildings are not impressing anyone!

As our assets increase, our ardor wanes. The Church's most dynamic century occurred when it owned not an acre of real estate. It was so busy spreading the Gospel that it didn't have time to waste in raising money for bricks and mortar. Its members raised money instead to aid the poor Christians in Jerusalem and to support their worldwide missionary outreach.

There seems to be a direct relationship between the waning of God's power and the building of church edifices. Take the Dark Ages for an example. There has never been another period when the Holy Spirit was so handicapped to move freely as during those centuries! The church of that day was full of corruption, including some church leaders who raced horses in Rome and fathered illegitimate children in Germany. During that period of starving masses, the church devoted herself to the erection of ornate chapels, decorated by famous artists. Used as tourist attractions in Europe today, they should stand as reminders to us that when heavenly things become obscure, "men of the cloth" usually turn to an interest in the tangible treasures of the earth—like a new ornate sanctuary, redecorated offices, or fountains on the parking lot.

This is one clergyman who wants to register heartsickness at the manner in which we continue to erect one building after another as status symbols of our success in the ministry. Time was when a pastor evaluated the effectiveness of his ministry by such things as human lives loved and converted; now, it seems, the yardstick by which success is measured is the buildings built and air conditioned.

It has taken a long time for me to get over the shock of hearing a minister some years back tell me of how he had gone to a church that was completely out of debt. He told me that he had made it a rule of his ministry that he would always keep his church in a building program; consequently, the first thing he did was to throw them into a quarter-of-a-million-dollar project. The shock has increased over the years, for I have heard that stated so many times that I have no further reason to think he was just one voice speaking.

The theory of this seems to be that people are loyal and committed to the church only when, and because, they are in debt. Nothing, it would seem, breeds loyalty like bank notes to be paid off. The whole matter has gotten ridiculously out of hand.

I recall a gigantic tomb of a church which was the recipient of a succession of ministers who all shared this philosophy. Each one of them added a building, large and imposing, until a full city block is now occupied. In a more prosperous era, stately homes surrounded this sacred spot, but they have long since been chopped into apartments for hippies and transients. A low-rent housing project cowers humbly nearby. The reverends and happy architects responsible for that church built it to last clear through the end of the millennium, but the community changed its mind about its life style in only thirty years. Now this church finds its massive buildings a veritable millstone about the necks of members who try to reach those who live around it. The poorer people who now comprise the community are scared to death by the opulence and grandeur of the exterior and are uncomfortable in the Gothic formality inside. A pity that earlier church leaders did not study the sociological patterns by which communities grow old and change constituents! The interest on the dollars invested in those bricks must still flow into the banker's pockets (a half million is still financed), even though funds are sorely needed for staff and programs to minister to those in the community.

The next time you sit down in a sanctuary, consider the amount of money it has cost for that space to be provided. Consider the number of *minutes* in a full week that space is used. As you wander down that eight-foot hallway, on your way to your classroom in the educational building, ponder the cost of an investment which is actually providing rooms for use 90 to 120 minutes a week. Drop by during the week, and look at the janitor waxing those floors, and ask yourself if this is really a businesslike way to run the greatest job on earth.

There is not a business in the nation which has the courage to invest as much as 50% of its capital in buildings to be used a handful of hours each week. The fact that the church has done so, and does not have its back to the wall in total financial bankruptcy, is proof positive that the Lord takes care of fools and His children.

Congregations need to face up to the responsibility they have to utilize their massive structures properly and more completely. I have discovered this particular matter is about as sore a point as any which can be broached with preachers. Their reaction is often emotionally charged and defensive. I feel the reason is an inner feeling of guilt that their church buildings are so fine and are used so little. There are some medium-sized towns in America where the First Church will possess the largest amount of floor space available in the entire community—and it literally is unused, except for offices, apart from Sundays and Wednesday evenings. Those thousands of square feet of educational space have been so built that they are almost impossible for use except as Sunday school classrooms. In a visit to one church, I discovered several of those rooms actually padlocked by dear women who were terrified someone might use them apart from their single hour of Bible Study on Sunday mornings; they obviously did not want their lovely hand-sewn *cushions* on the folding chairs to be soiled between Sundays.

Several years ago, I was invited to observe a conference of high-ranking Protestant denominational leaders in New York City. Bishops, presidents, and superintendents of various communions of the Northeast were to conduct a roundtable discussion. Their remarks went on for two hours: they were deploring the complete immorality of churches who were camping on five acres or so of valuable land in a crowded area which had used up all available ground. They concluded that the time had come to declare war on churches who used their buildings for three hours a week and could find no further use for them.

Shortly after that, I spent a fruitless two weeks trying to find a two-acre tract of land for a church site in a New Jersey county across the Hudson from Manhattan. Frustrated by failure, I secured an appointment with the head of the County Planning Commission. After listening to my problem, he smiled as he said, "Reverend, there hasn't been that much bare land in this county since the Second World War ended, except for the county airport. When we finally chop that up in another five or ten years, I predict it will sell for more than a half-million dollars an acre! You are about fifty years too late to be building churches in this county."

As I drove home on the Garden State Parkway, my mind reviewed the unbroken expanse of wall-to-wall humanity which stretches from Arlington, Virginia, to Boston, Massachusetts. "Megalopolis": thousands of urban centers, crushing into each other, causing land to disappear forever for first-time use. Here stand the planned cities, designed by pagan men who have provided every facility except places for the worship of God. Here are the planned high-rise apartments where eight hundred families live without a single room in the structure devoted to the adoration of Christ.

Demographers tell us the megalopolises of this last quarter-century will gradually emerge in patterns which will connect Minneapolis to Buffalo, New Orleans to

San Antonio and Dallas, St. Louis to Denver, and Mexico to Canada along the Pacific. The population of the United States will probably double in the next thirty years, requiring my denomination alone to double the number of local churches—*just to stay equal in witness to what we are doing today.* My denomination began church-building programs in 1845, and in 125 years it has amassed 35,000 units; now it must erect 35,000 more in only thirty years to "stay even."

Back in the golden age, frequently Mr. Smith donated the plot of land for the new church, and all businessmen gave cut prices to the church for materials needed to build it. Often the contractor did the job on a cost-plus-2% basis, and some men would donate all or a part of their labor costs.

Not any more! One building contractor in one of my barroom conversations told me that he loved to land a contract for a church building; there was more profit in that, he said, than in almost any other type of building, since usually there was not anyone to really check up on the prices he charged. Unions now make sure every artisan is paid full price. Sellers of land couldn't care less whether it is going to be used by a church or by Chrysler; they just want top dollar on their speculative investment.

A simple mathematical calculation is all it takes to validate the fact that, if the church does not wake up to its problem, it may well have priced itself out of existence in the United States! To buy two-acre tracts of land at today's prices for church sites and build 35,000 two-hundred-member-capacity "first units" on them at today's prices *would cost over seventeen and one-half billion dollars* for my denomination alone. Add interest rates varying from 7 to 9 percent, and the figure soars to a possible *twenty-seven billion dollars!* Realize that building costs are rising at an astonishing rate, that land is never going to be as cheap again as it is now, and the problem becomes even more astronomical.

Quiz: why do we have our present educational buildings? Answer: because a man at the beginning of the nineteenth century devised a plan by which all people gathered at *one time* and in *one building* for Bible study! That plan has been refined and refined, but it is still the same basic concept presented in 1800.

Buildings are determined by programs. They change only when the programs in them change. We are using a 170-year-old antique in the kitchen! Is there no other way to conduct Bible study apart from building behemoths? What about the real estate church members own or rent as dwellings? Could not Bible study be decentralized, using countless kitchen tables and living rooms as a base of operation? Could not children meet at various after-school hours, adults at evening periods, thus saving thousands of dollars poured into a church plant? Lives there a body of men and women who would dare to show the rest of us the way out?

Theaters are usually empty during the daytime on weekdays and on Sunday mornings. Could they be used for worship services? Is it not time to agree that public school buildings could well be a part of the answer to our dilemma? Would there be any significant violation of church and state if school buildings were *rented at a reasonable figure* to community churches for services held after 4:30 p.m. on weekdays, and on weekends?

At least one planned city in Maryland is experimenting with a scheme providing only one building devoted to religious activity. This one large edifice contains offices for all pastors in the city; individual rooms are rented by the hour and are of varying sizes to accommodate groups of various congregations.

Our experimental church in Houston has studied the need of the community and discovered that a great need will exist during the next fifteen years for child care facilities. By devising multi-purpose buildings, we now offer day care facilities for approximately 200 pre-school children during weekdays. Then we will be able to use the same space for Bible study classes on Sunday. In place of a sanctuary, unused except for two hours a week, we are building a multi-purpose room which will include all the necessary accoutrements for worship, cafeteria, roller skating, basketball, coffee house, theater, and large spaces which will be capable of being converted into small rooms by the use of movable walls for Sunday school. The entire church plant, including parking facilities will accommodate 950 members for worship and Bible study, and 200 pre-schoolers during the week. Most important, the revenue from the day care operation will pay for much of the cost of land and buildings. Church offerings can be invested in *people*. This pattern, adapted to similar areas, would make it possible for many new churches to have buildings without a heavy investment of funds.

Those who feel (sometimes violently) that all "God's buildings" can and should be paid for by the tithes and offerings of members need to be challenged to stop their fuzzy thinking! There is an old Book that makes it crystal clear that all man is and possesses belongs lock, stock, and barrel to Jesus Christ when He becomes Lord of life. If we can understand this, perhaps we can stimulate some extremely gifted Christian men in the world of real estate, business, and finance to begin to use their *minds* as well as their *checkbooks* for the Lord.

That is precisely what the building problem of the church is going to require: some dedicated, Spirit-filled laymen who can devise methods by which the church can either combine its need for space with something else which can pay the bills, or a program of training and worship which will permit the congregation to exist without any property at all. A layman is simply reneging on his stewardship when he tithes and teaches a Sunday school class for the Lord and then uses his divinely given intelligence simply for himself, to make investments which give him personal

171

profits of sizable proportions. If he can do that for himself, why should he not be doing it *for the Lord?* One layman in Minnesota developed a string of restaurants which have become a national chain, for the express purpose of providing immense sums for a Christian movement in which he was interested. A few months of his life invested in setting up that program will provide money for the Lord's work for several generations! Would it have been more "Christian" for him to make all that profit himself and then just *tithe* the income from it?

What could be done during the next thirty years if some of God's men who build shopping centers would develop each one with a combination room which could house secular activities during the week, yet be given over primarily for the use of a church, or churches, in the community on the weekend? Why could he not include a room to be provided free of charge to a pastor for use in counseling employees and customers about personal needs? Christian businessmen building apartments might well consider making one apartment in each development a chapel, available to community churches to use as an outreach center.

One large apartment project in Houston will soon be erected with 1,500 apartments. It will have its own bar, golf putting green, tennis courts, swimming pool, shopping center, child-care center, and a full-time recreation director. It will, in essence, become a microcosm of humanity superimposed upon the surrounding community; tenants in it will turn over at a rate approximating 110% each year. How much chance will a local church have of cracking that situation, being constructed without so much as a thought about the need for religious life within the complex? Those tenants will, by the sheer force of their surroundings, never become familiar with the life of the area beyond their own lavish layout. Tragically, one of the men primarily involved in the entire scheme is a leading churchman. One simple act of stewardship on his part might have provided the Gospel to over 4,000 people each year!

Perhaps some day soon a miracle will happen, and a group of laymen in Christendom will decide the time has come to let God into their motel chains, hotels, shopping centers, great office buildings, and businesses. When their time comes, there may be multiple solutions for churches who now pour half their money into mortar and are thus stripped of funds which might have been used to equip a mighty army of Christians to carry the battle to the lost. Until that time, we will go on dissipating much of our income for overhead expenses, for buildings used a few minutes each week. Only eternity will reveal how many people went to an eternal hell because we did so!

Appendixes

APPENDIX A
TOUCH Monthly Report

TOUCH Ministry .... Date ......

Director ....

A. List of church members involved in ministry:

....
....
....
....
....
....

List additional names on back if necessary.

B. Goals for next month:

	1st wk.	2nd wk.	3rd wk.	4th wk.
No. meetings held				
No. church members involved				
No. outsiders ministered to				
No. times Christ presented				
No. decisions for Christ				

C. Seekers needing follow up:

....
....
....
....
....

List additional names on back if needed.

D. List the names and addresses of all *new* people
   you have TOUCHed.

....
....
....

TURN IN one copy of report by first Sunday of each
month to TOUCH director. Keep one copy for your
records.

174

APPENDIX B

Confidential
PASTOR'S INFORMATION RECORD

Date: ....

Note: This information will not be released without your permission. It is helpful for your pastor to have this record, especially in a time of painful crisis in your life. If some questions seem too personal or do not fit your situation, simply omit them.

(Please print.)

Name .... Birthday .../.../...

Address .... Zip.... Telephone ..-....

I. CHILDHOOD

Father

Occupation?........... Living?................

Where?............... Christian?.............

Was your relationship close? ....

Mother

Did she work?......... Living?................

Where?.............. Christian?.............

Was your relationship close? ....

Brothers and sisters:

Name	Check one: Older	Check one: Younger	Living?	Where?	Christian?	Are you close?

II. EDUCATION

Name of school	Dates attended	Major	Minor	Degrees

III. ADULT LIFE

Military service:

Branch	Highest rank	Dates served	Skills, tasks	Medals

Are you now in a reserve unit? . . . .

Reserve branch	Present rank	Times for present duty requirements	Nature of your tasks

Business or professional life:

Name of firm . . . .

Nature of your work . . . . Title. . . . . . .

Business address . . . . Telephone . .-. . . . . .

    Concerning calls from your pastor while at work:

    ☐ Any time ☐ None, please

    ☐ Only in emergency

    Best time to call: Between hours of . . . .

    Are you free for lunch some times? . . . .

    Do you travel?. . . . . . To what areas, cities?. . . . . .

. . . .

Family life:

Spouse's name . . . .

Occupation. . . . . Birthday . ./. ./. . .

    Anniversary date: . ./. . Is he/she a Christian?. .

                   month day

    If he/she belongs to a church other than yours,

    state: . . . .

        Name   City

Previous churches you have belonged to:

Name of church	Dates attended	Positions held	Status: Active	Status: Inactive	Status: Attended
1.					
2.					
3.					

Present positions you hold in this church:

. . . .

Confidential
Children:

Page Three

Name	Age	Christian?	Church member?	In school? Give name:	Year of school	Lives at home?	If not, where?

Evaluate your relationships with the children: (omit if not applicable)

I am closest to: (name) ....

I have the poorest relationship with: (name) ......

I worry most about: (name) ....

I consider my relationship with the children to be:
- ☐ Deeply rooted in love
- ☐ Average
- ☐ Something we struggle to improve

Do you have a family altar in your home?
- ☐ Yes ☐ No
- ☐ Occasionally

All participate except: ....

Describe its nature: Amount of time, when scheduled, materials used: ....
....
....

IV. GENERAL INFORMATION

What other organizations do you belong to?
(Civic, government, social, lodges [degrees?], professional societies, etc.) ....
....

What special honors have come to your life? ......
....
....

IV. GENERAL INFORMATION (continued)

What are your special hobbies, interests? Your recreations? . . . .
. . . .
. . . .
. . . .

Where have you visited in your travels? . . . .
. . . .
. . . .

What are your skills in the field of music? . . . .
. . . .
. . . .

What are your personal goals, to be realized if possible within the next five years? . . . .
. . . .
. . . .
. . . .
. . . .

You may use the rest of this page to share any other information you would like your pastor to know.

. . . .
. . . .
. . . .
. . . .
. . . .
. . . .
. . . .
. . . .
. . . .
. . . .
. . . .
. . . .
. . . .
. . . .
. . . .

QUESTIONNAIRE

1. At what age were you converted?.... In what place? ....

2. Was your conversion: ☐ dramatic ☐ remembered ☐ not well-remembered

3. Have you: ☐ seldom doubted it ☐ never doubted it; or do you: ☐ never think about it

4. Were you to die right now, would you be with Christ? ☐ yes ☐ no ☐ not sure

5. Did you join the church *before* or *after* your conversion? ☐ after ☐ before

6. Has your spiritual growth since then been ☐ in spurts ☐ gradual ☐ slow ☐ connected with crises ☐ connected with a specific activity; (describe) ....
....

7. Do you have a consistent, daily, personal quiet time? ☐ yes ☐ no

8. Is your home life ☐ deeply related to Christ's presence ☐ casually related to Christ's presence

9. When the word "church" is spoken, is your first mental image that of: ☐ a building ☐ a program ☐ worship service ☐ other members

10. Your *present* pattern of participation:
Attend S. S. ☐: weekly ☐ bi-weekly ☐ monthly ☐ seldom ☐
Why? ....

Attend a.m. worship ☐: weekly ☐ bi-weekly ☐ monthly ☐ seldom ☐
Why? ....

Attend p.m. worship ☐: weekly ☐ bi-weekly ☐ monthly ☐ seldom ☐
Why? ....

Attend Wed. prayer mtg. ☐: weekly ☐
bi-weekly ☐ monthly ☐ seldom ☐
Why? . . . .

11. What "gifts" has God given you, which should
be utilized for Him?
List all you possess. Don't worry about *how* they
could be used, or if present church structures
have a place for them!
Examples: "Work best with my hands." "Have
ability in legal matters." "Do well with investments." "Am able to supervise people." "Am able
to teach." "Am able to train others." "Love to
entertain."
(Take some time to complete this!) . . . .
. . . .
. . . .
. . . .
. . . .
. . . .

Bibliography

Briscoe, D. Stuart. *Where Was the Church When the Youth Exploded?* Grand Rapids: Zondervan Publishing House, 1972.

Culpepper, Charles, Sr. *The Shantung Revival.* Dallas: Evangelism Division, Baptist General Convention of Texas, 1968.

Edge, Findley. *The Greening of the Church.* Waco: Word Books, 1972.

Gardner, John W. *Self-Renewal.* New York: Harper and Row, 1964.

Girard, Robert C. *Brethren, Hang Loose.* Grand Rapids: Zondervan Publishing House, 1972.

Grubb, Norman. *Touching the Invisible.* Fort Washington: Christian Literature Crusade, 1966.

Halverson, Richard C. *Be Yourself . . . and God's.* Grand Rapids: Zondervan Publishing House, 1972.

————. *How I Changed My Thinking About the Church.* Grand Rapids: Zondervan Publishing House, 1972.

Haney, David P. *Renew My Church.* Grand Rapids: Zondervan Publishing House, 1972.

————. *The Idea of the Laity.* Grand Rapids: Zondervan Publishing House, 1973.

Howse, W. L. and Thommason, W. O. *A Dynamic Church.* Nashville: Convention Press, 1969.

Murray, Ian H. *The Forgotten Spurgeon.* London: The Banner of Truth Trust, 1966.

Neighbour, Ralph W. *The TOUCH of the Spirit.* Nashville: Broadman Press, 1972.

————. *Witness, Take the Stand!* Dallas: Evangelism Division, Baptist General Convention of Texas, 1967.

Richards, Lawrence O. *A New Face for the Church.* Grand Rapids: Zondervan Publishing House, 1970.

————. *Youth Ministry.* Grand Rapids: Zondervan Publishing House, 1972.

Stephens, Bill. "The World of TOUCH," *People*. Nashville: The Sunday School Board of the Southern Baptist Convention, October, 1970.

Trueblood, Elton. *The Incendiary Fellowship*. New York: Harper and Row, 1967.

Wagner, C. Peter. *A Turned-on Church in an Uptight World*. Grand Rapids: Zondervan Publishing House, 1971.

Watson, G. D. "Others May, You Cannot." Westchester, Illinois: Good News Publishers.

Woodson, Leslie H. *Evangelism for Today's Church*. Grand Rapids: Zondervan Publishing House, 1972.